The Literature of Cinema

ADVISORY EDITOR: **MARTIN S. DWORKIN**
INSTITUTE OF PHILOSOPHY AND POLITICS OF EDUCATION
TEACHER'S COLLEGE, COLUMBIA UNIVERSITY

THE LITERATURE OF CINEMA presents a comprehensive selection from the multitude of writings about cinema, rediscovering materials on its origins, history, theoretical principles and techniques, aesthetics, economics, and effects on societies and individuals. Included are works of inherent, lasting merit and others of primarily historical significance. These provide essential resources for serious study and critical enjoyment of the "magic shadows" that became one of the decisive cultural forces of modern times.

The Photodrama

Henry A. Phillips

ARNO PRESS & THE NEW YORK TIMES

New York • 1970

109082

Reprint Edition 1970 by Arno Press Inc.
Reprinted from a copy in The Museum of Modern Art Library
Library of Congress Catalog Card Number: 70-124032
ISBN 0-405-01632-8
ISBN for complete set: 0-405-01600-X
Manufactured in the United States of America

THE AUTHORS' HAND-BOOK SERIES

THE PHOTODRAMA

THE PHILOSOPHY OF ITS PRINCIPLES, THE NATURE
OF ITS PLOT, ITS DRAMATIC CONSTRUCTION
AND TECHNIQUE ILLUMINED BY
COPIOUS EXAMPLES

TOGETHER WITH

A COMPLETE PHOTOPLAY AND A GLOSSARY

MAKING THE WORK

A PRACTICAL TREATISE

BY

HENRY ALBERT PHILLIPS

Author of "The Plot of the Short Story," "Art in Short Story Narration,"
Formerly of Staff of Pathé Frères, Successful Contestant in
Vitagraph-Sun Contest

INTRODUCTION BY

J. STUART BLACKTON

Pioneer Manufacturer and Producer and Secretary of The Vitagraph
Company of America

THE STANHOPE-DODGE PUBLISHING COMPANY
LARCHMONT, NEW YORK, U. S. A.

The William G. Hewitt Press
Brooklyn, New York

CONTENTS

CHAPTER   PAGE

INTRODUCTION ix

FOREWORD xv

PART I.—THE PRINCIPLES OF THE PHOTODRAMA.

I.—A NEW MEDIUM OF ARTISTIC EXPRESSION 27
The Premise of All Art; the Battle of New Standards; the Drama of the Eye; Not "Moving Pictures"; All the World's the Stage; a Field Without Limitations.

II.—DIFFERENTIATION 32
How Photodrama Differs from Stage Drama in Construction, Technique and Expression; Also from Fiction Construction and Narration in General and the Short Story and Novel in Particular.

III.—PARTS OF THE PHOTOPLAY AND THEIR PURPOSES 39
Title; Synopsis; Cast of Characters; Author's Remarks; Scenario; the Scene; the Setting.

IV.—VARIOUS DEVICES—THEIR USE AND MISUSE 48
The Caption; the Insert; the Close-View; the Vision; Dialog; Breaking Up Long Scenes; Preserving the Illusion.

V.—VISUALIZATION 65
Its Relation to Action; Importance of Vocabulary; Literature; to Register; Interpretation; in Terms of Emotion; the Part of Imagination.

VI.—CHARACTERIZATION 75
Identity and Personality; Characteristics and Idiosyncrasies; Description and Delineation; Establishing Relationship; Motives; Expression; Contrasts.

CONTENTS

CHAPTER   PAGE

VII.—THEME, TREATMENT AND THE CENSOR 87
Morals and Ethics; Crime; National Board of
Censorship; Taste; Inspiration and Influence.

VIII.—RULES OF THE GAME 97
Duration and Number of Scenes; Perpetual
Motion; the "Now" Element; Effective Form;
Natural Laws; Scene Principle.

IX.—BROMIDES WORTH REPEATING .   .   . 107
The Virtue of Economy; Producing Policies;
Period and Costumes; Animals; Copyright and
Carbon Copies; Relation of Author's Work to
His Audience; to the Manufacturer; to His
Manuscript.

PART II.—THE PLOT OF THE PHOTODRAMA.

I.—WHAT PLOT MATERIAL IS .   .   . 119
The Plot Germ; the Premise Advanced; Ancient
Theme and Original Treatment.

II.—WHERE TO GET PLOT GERMS .   . 124
Observation; Reading; Employment of Facts;
the Daily Newspaper; Dangers; Propriety;
Originality; the "True Story"; Importance of
Notes; Titles; Plot Classification.

III.—BEGINNING WITH THE END .   . 132
Seeking the Climax; When to Begin the Photoplay; Ever-Forward Movement; the Live Beginning.

IV.—DEVELOPMENT AND CONTINUITY . . 138
Each Scene Contributes to the Climax; Element
of Time and Chronological Sequence; Problems
of Continuity; the Central Theme; the Return;
Instantaneous Sequence; Time Indicatives.

V.—THE CLIMAX AND COMPLETED PLOT . 146
Sequence and Consequence; Logical Cause and
Complete Solution; Sustained Climax; All
Expectations Fulfilled.

CONTENTS

CHAPTER   PAGE

PART III.—DRAMATIC CONSTRUCTION OF THE PHOTOPLAY.

I.—DRAMA AND PHOTODRAMA 150
Definition; Principles; Structure is Everything;
the Dramatic Idea; Emotion is the Secret;
Desire the Motive Power; Drama and Melodrama.

II.—DRAMATIC EXPRESSION 155
The Laws of Movement and Action; Character
and Motive; Relation to Audience and Character; Dramatic versus Dynamic; Realism;
Romanticism and Idealism.

III.—SEQUENCE AND SUSPENSE 161
Cause and Effect; Effects Due to Arrangement;
the Raw Coincidence; Suspense Motors: Battle
of Opposing Motives; Motive as Well as Idea.

IV.—THE POTENTIAL SITUATION . . . 166
Contrast; Situation's Relation to Audience;
Harvesting Situations; Peril and Death; Climax
and Punch.

V.—UNITY PLUS HARMONY EQUALS EFFECT. 175
Questions in the Mind of the Audience;
Reason; Truth; Struggle; Solution; the Title;
Harmony Values.

PART IV.—FORMS AND TYPES OF THE PHOTOPLAY.

I.— 185
Drama and Melodrama; Tragedy; Comedy;
Other Forms; "Split Reel"; Short Play; Long
Play; Spectacle; Adaptations; Play Divisions.

II.—A SPECIMEN PHOTOPLAY 192
The Effectiveness of Typography; "The Salt of
Vengeance,"—a Short Play Drama. .

GLOSSARY 212
The Most Used Terms Defined, with Many
Suggestions for Revision and Alternative Terms.

INTRODUCTION

AS one of the pioneers in the most wonderful art-science of the age—the motion picture industry—the writer feels doubly qualified perhaps to throw some light upon a subject equally interesting to author and producer.

A few years ago to the uninitiated "moving pictures" spelt little more than pantomime, buffoonery or sensational catch-penny device. To-day, there are few who maintain this view, and they are the unenlightened; for to the vast majority of those familiar with the art and interested in its progress, the word has become symbolic of things important and far-reaching.

Literature is literally the basic foundation upon which the already gigantic edifice of picturedom has risen.

Ten or twelve years ago picture manuscripts were unknown—office boys, clerks, camera operators, any one with an "idea" furnished the material from which motion pictures were produced. Plot was unknown, technique did not exist, and literary and constructive quality was conspicuous by its absence. The art, however, developed rapidly. It was found possible to do more than portray outdoor scenes of moving trains and other objects, or simple pantomimes with exaggerated gesture *à la Française*. Methods were discovered and evolved whereby powerfully dramatic scenes could be reproduced, subtilty of expression in either serious or humorous vein could be communicated to numberless people—their emotions played upon, laughter or tears evoked at will—in other words, the Silent Drama was born.

Classic and standard literature was then reproduced in photodrama. Shakespeare, Dickens, Thackeray, Scott and Hugo became known to millions of people whose previous acquaintance with their famous works was either very slight or non-existent. It was at this stage, when literature was combined with other arts allied in picture production, that the real impetus was given and the triumphant onward march of the world's greatest educator and entertainer commenced.

To-day, millions are invested in great in-

dustrial plants for the creation and manufacture of the wordless drama; thousands of people rely upon it as their sole maintenance and
profession. Millions upon millions of men,
women and children all over the world look
upon this form of entertainment as their principal recreation and, incidentally, are being
unconsciously educated to understand and appreciate the higher forms of art.

Bernard Shaw says: "The great artist is he
who goes a step beyond the demand and, by
supplying works of a higher beauty and a
higher interest than have yet been perceived,
succeeds after a brief struggle in adding this
extension of sense to the heritage of the race."

There is no doubt that the works of higher
beauty and interest accomplished by the real
artists in the motion picture profession have
been widely productive of the "extension of
sense" above quoted.

All this brings us to the practical purpose
of this discussion—the dissemination among
those who write of the intelligence that a new
and fruitful field is open for the works of
their pens. The short-story writer who gets
from one hundred to five hundred dollars

for magazine stories can get a similar amount from the picture manufacturers; the authors of international fame, who make thousands in royalties, can make thousands more from picture royalties—and in every case without interfering with their magazine or book rights. In fact, the greatest advertising a novel could receive would be a preliminary exhibition all over the world in pictures.

Many of the best modern authors have already gone into this field and many more will. For the day has arrived when, in addition to producing well-known plays and successful books, there is a need for big original features, especially written for pictorial presentation.

The motion picture has narrowed the field of the playwright, but there is another and broader pasture awaiting both the play and fiction writer when he has mastered the technique of the "life portrayal."

It is the writer's belief that a gripping, compelling story, hitherto unknown and unpublished, *properly picturized* and bearing the name of one of the best known writers of modern fiction, would be a greater success artistically and financially than a revived popular play or "best seller." The words "properly picturized" emphasized above are significant.

The motion picture manufacturer stands to the author in the position of publisher—he needs you—you need him. There are good and bad publishers. You, whose name is an asset. would not deal with a publisher of questionable methods; ergo, when seeking out a market for your work, deal with none but the highest class and best and old-established motion picture concerns.

Picturedom is looked upon by many as the New Eldorado. Many misguided fools are rushing in where experienced angels fear to tread. Many theatrical concerns are now "going into the moving picture business," and they blithely announce their intention to uplift the motion picture and show the public some real stage productions done in pictures. The few that have come to light so far have been very sad affairs, as is but natural. The average theatrical man makes about the same brand of pictures as the average picture producer made five years ago. To quote again the invaluable Shaw, "Vital art work comes always from a cross between art and life."

The art of the picture is to convey an impression of absolute realism in a manner artistic. The theatrical stage manager has been proven to be utterly useless in picture production until he has unlearned all traditions of the stage and acquired an entirely new technique. It is unfortunate that many stock-jobbing, security-selling schemes are being offered to investigators and the public under the magic "movie" name. Many royalties are being promised that will never be paid and of many of these cardboard houses great will be the fall thereof. "A word to the wise is sometimes money in pocket."

All summed up in a paragraph, the answer is, without a *story* motion pictures would be what they were styled at their inception—a novelty or a fad. So literature is indissolubly linked with the future and success of the greatest of the allied arts. The "life portrayal" or "thought visualized" is perhaps better than all "literature realized."

J. Stuart Blackton.

xiv

*The coarse passion of the Crowd
constitutes "What the public wants"
in the way of productions; the refined emotion of the artist must
discipline, guide and gratify it by his
appealing creations.*

FOREWORD

WRITERS of fiction and dramatic
literature have been less apt to re-
spond to the call of a new literary vocation,
than a world-wide public has been ready to
flock to the appeal of a new dramatic art.

A wonderful event has come to pass in the
annals of dramatic literature thru the development of cinematography. So wonderful in-
deed was this new addition to the art of
effective dramatic expression, that even after
a decade of existence, scarcely a dozen successful writers of literature had realized its
potentiality and had allied themselves with
the new drama.

The public's first recognition of cinematography was as a novel diversion. People
flocked to see these presentations that crudely

reproduced not merely static likenesses, but moving realities, just as they had appeared before the camera. In those early days only the elemental reproduction of moving objects was attempted. The photography was miserable; the presentation itself a blurred, eye-racking ordeal.

Luckily for the waning novelty, the possibilities for the trick picture were suddenly realized and cinematography took on a new lease of life. But once the wonder, amazement and speculation that surrounded the unnatural phenomena of these animated photographs wore off, they became deadly monotonous for the mature mind. Once again cinematography hovered near the abyss of oblivion.

Something significant, however, had transpired: the trick picture had blundered, as it were, into the realms of misadventure and laughter. Slap-stick farce supplemented and finally succeeded the trick picture. Cinematography as an entertainment acquired a tremendous commercial impetus immediately. In less than a year the puling infant became a healthy youngster, and the five-cent theater began to take its rightful place as "the poor man's playhouse."

Thus we have arrived at the beginnings of a need for a literature to provide for the screen portrayals. What had previously been the device of a moment or the conception of an hour, on the part of some ingenious—or ingenuous—director, together with the combined aid of all concerned, now became a matter of serious consideration in order more nearly to meet and to co-operate with the mechanical requirements of length of film, speed of operation and duration of projection. All products were "home-spun" and in no way belied their crude sources. In a very short while it was discovered that there were surprisingly few funny ideas and situations in real life. The comedy personalities of clever actors were worked to death trying to put something new into old, frowsy and threadbare saws.

But a world-old, child-young desire had been awakened. The now vast audiences wanted to be told a story—logical, dramatic, gripping, living! They did not quite realize— as they never do—what they were clamoring

for, and the producers had paused aghast, as
tho conscious of the new and Silent Drama
that stood at that moment on the threshold
of cinematography.

The first cinematograph stories were humorous. Most of them were pathetic—which
is the case when any but a story teller tries to
tell a funny story. The serious story was
attempted with even worse results. The arrogance of the trained writer of fiction or of
drama and the price of the producer were
still beyond conciliation.

The first borrowings may have come in taking excerpts from history to make the modest
spectacles that gave a new note to cinematography. Suffice it to say, that soon familiar
masterpieces of fiction and dramatic literature
began to appear. The moment that the ex-
haustless stores of literature were opened to
the needs of cinematography we may say that
the photodrama really had its inception. In
the voracious search for a story, borrowing
became more general, descending from the
greater to the lesser lights. At first, borrowings were looked upon by both authors and
publishers almost good-naturedly. Not until

the intrinsic commercial value of literary work, from a photodramatic point of view, became obvious was the virtue of the copyright called into effect.

Several successful suits by publishers brought the fear of the copyright into the producers' hearts. The scenario editor and the photoplaywright became a power from that time on.

All said and done, a large percentage of the photoplaywrights developed in the mechanico-commercial atmosphere of the early days of cinematography were bound to be limited in their range of vision, in their conception of artistic drama and in their ideas of the needs of the ever-widening audiences. From the five-cent show, with its audiences of crude farce- and melodrama-loving people of small or limited education, had sprung the million-dollar theaters, including the rich and poor, the learned and the ignorant, the young and the old in their vast, changing throng of patrons, demanding something always better.

Is it any wonder—with the heads of the companies becoming wealthy magnates by the hour—that many of them gave little thought to anything else but the income end of their wonderful business, forgetting the output almost to the point of killing the goose that laid the golden egg? Many of these men had not the slightest conception what the word drama meant; altho their employees had grown up with the business, yet they knew nothing of those more cultured professions of literature and drama. Drama to them meant only the production of so many feet of "pictures."

On the other hand, the consummate handlers of plots, the trained writers of fiction and dramatic literature, who had made writing their profession and had given years of their life to demonstrating their ability to make men laugh and cry and wait, by means of dramatic pictures on page or stage—they had stood aloof. The studio-bred photoplay-wright smiled indulgently as tho an insuperable barrier separated these literary mastodons from their preserves; the writers scanned the field arrogantly as tho viewing the common herd. Neither was giving the other his due.

It is true, many well-known writers have failed as photoplay technicians; but it is even more true that most photoplaywrights would fail as writers of fiction or stage drama.

Thus we arrive at our point: photoplay writing is a new profession, for the simple reason that the photodrama is a new form of dramatic expression, tho in many ways like, yet in even more ways differing from, either fiction or stage drama.

The studio-bred photoplaywright needs just as much to study and to learn the valued art of choosing, developing and completing the dramatic idea artistically, as the writer of fiction or stage drama needs to master the difficult and effective technique of the photoplay.

The photodrama is more sophisticated than either the writer of other forms of literature, who dabbles with it, or the studio-bred photoplaywright, who struggles with it, at first suspects. Each new test of illusion that is put to it has been met effectively, maintained realistically and completed convincingly—providing it has had the artistic co-operation of director, actors and appropriate scenic effects.

It was but a natural consequence that years of dearth of play material and practical apprenticeship should have brought to the surface many promising photodramatists from among the studios. While there have been a limited number of plays effective from a purely artistic standpoint, and depending thruout on emotional situations, there have been thousands upon thousands of productions, startling because of dynamic spectacles, with scarcely a dramatic suggestion outside of outlandish peril. The clash of souls is lost sight of in the orchestral crash of falling buildings; the climax in the struggle of a heroic spirit is hidden behind locomotives coming head-on and smashing themselves into junk; the pathetic twilight closing over some wonderful character depiction is lost in the glare of a bona-fide fire advertised to cost thousands of dollars. These are melodramatic sensations, not drama.

Just as the average person can seldom appreciate a startling sensation except for the first time, so we find producers, directors and audiences clamoring for something new and surpassing all that has gone before, resenting repetition or spectacles that are keyed below the highest pitched sensation they have already witnessed. One visit to the circus a year suffices most people; tho few of us are contented with a weekly attendance at the theater with the promise of a good drama. Dramatic revivals are always welcome.

And so we see the feverish daily change of program, and films that flare for a day and then, like the reams of cheap reading trash of the hour, are literally thrown into the wastebasket and justly perish.

Many problems have been met with wonderful facility in this new art. The actor, for instance, has had to mould himself to new requirements, demanding of him oftentimes a more exquisite art than the spoken drama comprehends. A vast number of actors have acquired something near perfection.

A power has risen in the production of the photoplay, however, that has often hampered the progress of the new drama. All authority, in too many instances, has been given to the director. Even tho the meaning of the word classic was as remote from his understanding as the study of astronomy, yet all manuscripts were subject to his interpretation, alteration and elimination, from "Lucile" to "Lear." Too often actors en masse have had no further intimation of what they were doing than the vociferous bellowings of a director beyond the camera. Thus was the writer deprived of his most necessary ally in the interpretation of his finer dramatic ideas. If many directors cannot "see," and possibly perceive every scene and situation of a manuscript with all their five senses, they have been known to return it to the author as "impossible for production." In true drama our five senses—in photodrama but one, sight—merely act as the agent of the emotions, the real participant in the drama.

The photodrama is bound to be taken seriously in the end. We have theaters, we have actors, manufacturing plants, we have a world-wide audience—but no vital drama worth mentioning yet. When we are supplied with good plays the millennium of the photodrama will begin, which, in its universality, will eclipse anything known in the realms of artistic expression. The photodrama needs thinkers, not tinkers. There must come writers with ideas as well as methods. The future has room only for swayers of world-wide emotion, and not mere footage producers.

The trained writer has only a slight advantage over the untrained writer, because he must reject all his well-grounded rules of fiction and dramatic technique. The novice has a better chance in photoplay writing than in any other field of expression, providing he is mentally and temperamentally equipped to take it up.

Photoplay writing is bound to become a dignified profession despite the obloquy that seemed to rest upon it for so long. But the photoplaywright must elevate himself thru his artistic product and thru a demand for recognition of meritorious work by appropriate compensation and also by credit of his name to appear on the screen as author of his plays.

It is to further these high aims in the realization that the photodrama needs students earnest in their desire to become honest artisans and true artists—that this book has been written by an ardent student of the new art.

HENRY ALBERT PHILLIPS.

May 18, 1914.

PART I

THE PRINCIPLES OF THE PHOTODRAMA

The writer of the Silent Drama must portray emotions that may be felt by all mankind, and create heart-beats that may be heard round the world.

CHAPTER I

A New Medium of Artistic Expression

THE PREMISE OF ALL ART; THE BATTLE OF NEW STANDARDS; THE DRAMA OF THE EYE; NOT "MOVING PICTURES"; ALL THE WORLD'S THE STAGE; A FIELD WITHOUT LIMITATIONS.

IN all expressions of true art we find the portrayal of a message from the soul, mind and emotions of one man to those of his fellows. The message may be graven in stone, wrought in iron, blended in color, soaring in song, poured thru a pen, or spoken from the stage. If it be art none may pass by without a portion of it entering his soul and enriching his experience.

There is one essential condition, however, that precedes all participation in, and mutual enjoyment of, art—only true believers may enter the shrine of complete illusion. The observer, the reader, the listener, the participator in a work of art, must concentrate the attention of his body, mind and soul upon the emotional message it contains, regardless of the artificial mediums employed in giving it material existence. For art consists simply in an endeavor to express thru an outward and visible symbol some inward and spiritual truth, or struggle.

All new and unfamiliar forms of art, therefore, are subject to superficial criticism, if not ridicule, on the part of the uninitiated, who either fail, or refuse, to see the underlying truth interpreted by a work of art. Upon being shown one of the splendid marbles of Angelo they see but a piece of chiseled stone and not the wonderful vision that inspired the artist. To them one of Turner's symphonies of color is but a daubed canvas.

But once let appreciation of art values become part of a people's understanding, and the glories of a new and more wonderful world is opened to them, which brings us to the conclusion that there is a division of opinion regarding even the Fine Arts—some of which are patronized by the few, others are participated in by the many. Among the latter we find the devotees of fiction and dramatic literature far outnumbering all others. The reason, without doubt, for the wider popular approval of these two mediums of artistic expression lies in their portrayal of a segment of life with all the vicissitudes, settings, characters and contributing elements that lead to its dramatic climax, as opposed to the single static incident that the artist has limned in stone or wood or on canvas.

Stage drama takes even a step in advance of fiction literature in its approximation of realistic illusion. The characters of the play become the breathing, living, walking and talking persons conceived by the playwright and anticipated by the audience. Audiences laugh and weep, rejoice and sigh, despite themselves, wherever good stage drama is offered.

Thus we come to the inception and introduction of a new medium of artistic expression that is destined to be numbered among the Fine Arts. While the Photodrama is closely allied and dependent upon both Fiction and Dramatic Literature, yet it has a construction, an expression, and a production so uniquely its own that it is even more unlike than like its allied sources. The Photodrama is notable, too, in being science's first contribution to the Fine Arts.

The Photodrama has had to fight its battle of the new standards. The day was when we scoffed at the possibility of a mere animated photograph making an artistic appeal to us sufficient to stir our emotions. The conquest of the lighter emotions is already a reality, as any one may learn who will take the trouble to step into a photoplay theater while a good comedy is being run. But the supreme test of the appeal of art—the drama that loosens the treasured tears of a self-conscious, conservative audience—is still the unattained, but attainable, goal of the new profession.

Too often the message of fiction or stage drama is limited, by the printed or spoken word, to the understanding of one's own people; but the drama of the screen is told in terms of world-wide action, spelt in a tremor of world-old emotion, and writ in the simple language of the human heart—regardless of culture or color, clime or creed. He who has eyes to see may readily understand.

In Photodrama, as in real life, we are never permitted to reverse the hand of Time and relive the deeds of yesterday—except we pass thru the gateway of visions and dreams.

CHAPTER II

DIFFERENTIATION

HOW PHOTODRAMA DIFFERS FROM STAGE DRAMA IN CONSTRUCTION, TECHNIQUE AND EXPRESSION; ALSO FROM FICTION CONSTRUCTION AND NARRATION IN GENERAL AND THE SHORT STORY AND THE NOVEL IN PARTICULAR.

THE very first impulse that comes to the photoplaywright, as a true exponent of literary art, must be stifled—he cannot clothe his message in glowing words that will ravish the ear and please the eye of an esthetic public. Rather, he must construct a silent, technically wordless picture. He must smother his vocabulary under a mass of technique. He must hide the light of his diction under a bushel of "business."

32

Nevertheless, there must be the message to radiate, the story to tell, the gratifying material for entertainment. Granted an idea worth artistic exploitation, there remains the exercise of one of the most difficult processes known to literary or dramatic construction.

A photoplay is composed primarily of mechanical units, technically termed reels. A full reel consists of 1,000 feet of film and occupies approximately twenty minutes to display its contents upon the screen. By contents, we mean to include everything that is projected: trade-mark frame of manufacturer, including title of play and name of the author; cast of characters, with Board of Censorship notice at the end. The foregoing take approximately two minutes of valuable time and are merely incidental to the play. They concern the writer only in so far as they act as limitations. The essential photodrama itself includes portrayal of dramatic action of the characters; printed words contained in captions and inserted dialog; close-views for the purpose of emphasis; inserted printed matter bearing upon the unfolding of the story.

We find a distinct advantage in the con-

33

struction of the short stage play over that of
the short photoplay in the fact that the former
permits us approximately as long a time for
its single scene as we are allowed for the entire photoplay composed of from 25 to 60
scenes! Again, the short stage play is merely
episodical in an intensive sense, developing a
single dramatic situation to an immediate and
effective climax; while the short photoplay is
usually expansive in character, comparable to
the wider boundaries of the short story in selecting a supreme dramatic moment in the life
or lives of characters and portraying even the
remote cumulative incidents that began, con-
tributed to and compelled the climax, and possibly containing many situations, tho of lesser power than the climax itself. Aside from
the incidental employment of a mob now and
then, we may say that a vital characteristic
of the short stage play is economy, often two
and seldom more than five characters appearing in the play. Because of its multiplicity of
scenes, however, the short photoplay normally
includes the employment of many extra characters who establish and naturalize settings,
and seldom employs less than five important

characters, for the reason that frequent change of scene is necessary to photoplay development and effect.

(EXAMPLE 1.) In a short photoplay it may be necessary for our hero to visit his club, to gamble and to lose the money that he is holding in trust. While he and the villain, his opponent in the game, are the two principal characters, it is essential to introduce many others to make the club-setting natural. We might call these "setting characters."

(EXAMPLE 2.) We must always take into consideration those scenes that act as a foil for those in which our principal characters appear in their important situations. Photoplay scenes without the prop of dramatic dialog begin to lose power after being sustained for two or three minutes. New power is provided by reverting to another scene that has a direct cumulative bearing upon the scene in hand. With but two characters, or only a small group that must be kept together for effect, quick changes would keep the characters moving unnaturally fast.

An examination of the three-act, or long, stage play and a comparison with either short or long photoplay, likewise disclose some advantages in favor of the stage drama. Each act of the long play allows the playwright approximately forty minutes in which to at-tain a desired effect, or about one hour and twenty minutes of combined action in all. By means of the condensed method and rapid action of photoplay drama, we may often get a three-act play into a single reel of photoplay action, while a solid evening's entertainment may include several short plays, and one long one, equivalent in itself to a meaty drama.

The great advantage of photodrama over stage drama, however, lies in the playwright's privilege to fill in all essential action of the most infinitesimal character in exactly the order and degree of its occurrence, so that the spectator gets everything first-hand and not thru hearsay. Furthermore, the photoplay begins at the beginning of things essential.

(EXAMPLE 3.) Stage drama, thru the use of a few well-chosen phrases, will often make clear to the audience the relationship between characters and the cause for the struggle that is the basis of the play. Photoplay construction takes us back to the causal act, tho it may have happened months before the opening of the bigger situations.

The great problem that confronts the photo-playwright is how to make his story convincing without words, how to interpret every emotion into pure action. He must learn the truth of that axiom which states that "actions speak louder than words."

With fiction construction and expression, the photoplay has much in common. The short photoplay, as we have pointed out, is expanded to practically the same degree as the short story, while the multiple-reel, or long photoplay, has within its scope the complete and satisfactory dramatization of the novel or many-volumed literary work, thus enriching the dramatic field with new forms of surpassing material which must forever have been denied millions of people who abhor reading even the glorious treasures of fiction literature.

The two fields—of fiction writing and photoplay writing—diverge into opposite directions the moment we discuss the narration of one and the visualization of the other. In fiction narration, we resort unequivocally to words to express our inmost vision and weave our story; in the photoplay our words merely indicate the line of action. The effectiveness to be gained thru descriptive writing is barred to us; we must confine our description to a line at the head of each scene. Fine paragraphs on introspection, or mental agony, or deep feeling are helpless, unless they have their counterpart in vivid action. Artistic narration is a handicap; expressive vocabulary is essential. We must express ourselves, then, in terms of action rather than in periods of rhetoric.

But does not the absence of the spoken word make it easier to give expression to the universal language of the heart? All motives and emotions must be made to appear on the surface. Even sounds must be silently, yet effectively, portrayed. The music artist peoples the imagination of his audience with a glorious phantasmagoria. There is a music of vision that delights the beholder of motion and action, typifying life, health and sanity. We have only to give photoplay art its premise and we may find it ranked among the muses. In artistic photodrama we perceive with the ears of the heart and the soul, gifted, it would seem, with a new soul organ. The day of the skilled spectator must follow the dawn of the art of the ideal interpreter.

Here we do not want that mechanics of motion which labors and creaks, revealing the machine; but rather that poetry of silent action which translates itself emotionally into visualized motive and visible drama.

CHAPTER III

PARTS OF THE PHOTOPLAY AND THEIR PURPOSES

TITLE; SYNOPSIS; CAST OF CHARACTERS; AUTHOR'S REMARKS; SCENARIO; SCENE; SCENE-PLOT.

WE find the presentation of the photoplay in manuscript differing widely from that of both fiction and stage drama, in that it represents a mechanical point of view. Whereas the entire fiction manuscript is submitted verbatim as it will appear before the reader, and the stage play manuscript contains every word as it will be heard by the audience, the photoplay manuscript contains only a few lines of captions and possibly several inserts

39

which alone of the actual manuscript will appear on the screen.

The first item that appears on the manuscript, the title, is coming more and more to be regarded from its literary and story-fulfilling point of view. We must ever bear it in mind, however, chiefly as a commercial asset. First, will it attract and reach the pocketbook of the hesitating public and add a drawing power to the poster displayed in front of the theater? Second, will it successfully compete with the ever-increasing number of releases brought to the attention of the exhibitor to choose for his daily or weekly change of program? Third—and in a lesser degree—will it appeal to the photoplay editor because of its promise of high-class literary or dramatic material? It is possible in nine cases out of ten to combine all these desirable features, but not without careful thought.

The synopsis of the photoplay is something more than a mere synopsis, it is an abridgment, a condensation of the scene contents. To write a perfect synopsis requires the exercise of rare literary skill. By this is not meant rhetorical flow, but the power of such a choice and command of words that enables the writer to reduce possibly several thousand words of instructive scenario to a few hundred words of suggestive synopsis without missing a single essential point. There must be a style of telling the photoplay story that is terse, crisp and suggestive. There is a studio convention that seems to have limited the length of the synopsis to 250 words. It is unfair to make a hard-and-fast rule governing the synopsis, for the reason that most aspirants get an erroneous impression. Experience demonstrates that most clean-cut, vivid plots may be perfectly delineated in a synopsis of even less than 100 words. On the other hand, the power of the slight play made great thru pure dramatic artistry would suffer from a too brief synopsis. The refined emotional play free from all the coarser strain of exaggerated melodrama and sensational spectacle would sacrifice its finer points if it did not touch upon them and reveal their beauty in the synopsis. Employ as few words as you can to amplify and completely tell the abridged story of your play!

The synopsis is designed primarily for the

convenience of the editor or reader who takes up your manuscript with a view to its acceptability. The synopsis is its recommendation. If it does not tell him all its dramatic possibilities in a brief space, its opportunity is lost, for the editor seldom has time or inclination to peruse the scenario. Should the manuscript meet with acceptance, the synopsis is thereafter used as a guide for the director.

(EXAMPLE 4.) Showing how little side-lights are thrown on character, and shades of emotion may be revealed in the synopsis: "Frail, piquant Rosalie, with whom Malcolm is in love, is often piqued because he never comes to the point in anything. . . . Malcolm prefers to sit on the porch and dream of his coming deed. . . . Douglas is a doer of things and immediately carries out the music in his heart in appealing words."

The cast of characters should mention individual characteristics if possible and clearly show the relationships at a glance. The cast is for the convenience of the director in computing the number of players necessary, in selecting actors for the parts according to their talents and personal characteristics.

(EXAMPLE 5.) MALCOLM FRENCH . . . .
(Lead) . . . . In love with Rosalie; Artist, Dreamer.

ROSALIE . . . . (Ingénue-lead) . . . . Piquant, impatient, frail, flirtatious.

Characters that appear singly should be mentioned singly; those appearing in groups, or mobs, described en masse, so that the director may form at a glance a comprehensive idea of outlay in characters, costumes and possible character props.

There should be a distinct part of each photoplay manuscript known as "Author's Remarks." These should be brief and contain such helpful suggestions as a mention of the period of the play, its locale, where ideal locations may be found near particular studios, the need of extraordinary properties and where they might be obtained (possibly the author might have in his possession a coin, MS., or oddity), maybe the suggestion of specific actors whom you have in mind for important parts. Confine these remarks to 50 words or less.

The part of the manuscript next to appear is the scenario, or enumeration of scenes, including the respective action taking place in each. After numbering the scene, a single line is devoted to the description of the scene or setting. This is the only space permitted the writer for description, and one or two words are supposed to suffice unless he wishes a certain arrangement of setting that will have dramatic bearing on the development of the action.

(EXAMPLE 6.)   Scene 3—FRONT OF SHOP (Window plainly lettered: J. CADWALLADER— ANTIQUE JEWELS).

Despite the fact that it is the same in name as a division of stage drama, a photoplay scene is by no means identical with a stage play scene. An apt parallel may be drawn by saying that while a stage scene is all that is seen and acted in one setting without dropping the curtain, a photoplay scene is all of the setting and action that is photographed without stopping or changing the position of the camera. If the position of the camera is changed an inch, or if we should return to the same scene a score of times, viewing it from the identical point, it must bear another scene number and be treated as a new scene. There is one exception to this rule. When a scene is broken by an insert or a close-view we "continue" the scene, for the reason that the scene is not interrupted at all in the taking, the film being cut to insert either close-view or other inserted matter.

(EXAMPLE 7.) Scene 24.—INTERIOR PAWN-BROKER'S. Broker takes necklace from case, examines it, eyeing Douglas all the while, examines jewels with jeweler's glass, then turns, with shake of head: INSERT 4 . . . . "I DON'T RECEIVE STOLEN GOODS. GET OUT OR I'LL CALL THE POLICE!" Scene 24—(Continued). Douglas slinks out with a scowl.

It is presupposed that every scene set down in the manuscript is absolutely necessary, and by necessary we mean essential to the cumulative advancement of the play. The contents of the scene itself consists of the writer's process of visualizing his story thru appropriate directions for the movement of the characters and a description of the resultant action, vividly, tersely and suggestively *told in the present tense.* The same economical care should be practised in the selection of only essential material and the rejection of unessential details as one observes in the construction of the short story. While the writer is supposed to tell only what is to be done and not to presume even to suggest how, yet there

45

are many subtile emotions the perfect interpretation of which he may have in mind. A happy suggestion may often save the busy and hurried actor or director time, and express exactly what the writer has in mind instead of making it necessary to guess at his thoughts.

As the writer plans the effect to be produced by his completed play, so he must keep in mind a desired effect to be accomplished by each scene. The length of a scene is determined precisely by it attaining the single effect for which it was created. Thus a scene has a unity of its own which is comparable with that of the complete play: Introduction, or establishment of relationship sufficient for the audience to grasp the significance of the action; rising development; pronounced climax, which is the signal for its termination—for a scene never has a denouément. The succeeding scene always carries the play a step forward or higher.

(EXAMPLE 8.) Scene 52—ON THE BALCONY. Malcolm singing with his whole soul in his expression. Scene 53—JEWEL ROOM. Douglas still kneeling before the cabinet, suddenly pauses, his face contorted with painful memory.

Much confusion would be eliminated, and clearness and precision affected, if there were a change in terminology calling scenes "acts," for they are distinct units of action and definite and complete acts in the development of the play. The scene, as its etymology indicates, has primarily to do with the scenery or setting. The same scene is repeated over and over again, tho it always bears a new number. The same act is never repeated (except in facsimile in the vision scene), so that the consecutive numbering of acts from beginning to end of play would have a specific value, just as the consecutive numbering of repeated scenes is decidedly confusing.

SPECIAL NOTE.—In Part IV of this volume will be found one complete photoplay, embodying all points discussed in these chapters, and from which, in the main, illustrative examples have been chosen. A Glossary contains a modified definition of all technical terms employed.

Artifice is the edged tool of Art which, when wielded skilfully, may carve lines of life in a piece of clay and bring fame to the artificer; when handled clumsily it is sure to mar the material and may injure the hand of the artisan.

CHAPTER IV

VARIOUS DEVICES—THEIR USE AND MISUSE

THE CAPTION; THE INSERT; THE CLOSE-VIEW; THE VISION; DIALOG; BREAKING UP LONG SCENES; PRESERVING THE ILLUSION.

D O not seek to write photoplays that are sufficient in themselves and do not need the aid of tricks of the trade, devices or artifices. Such plays must need be crude because, even tho perfect in plot, they are bound to appear cut-and-dried, clipped and cured, and wanting in all those little human touches which by piercing the emotions and gaining the sympathies of the audience, do more than win the approbation of the mind. The impression that the perfect play is the one which can dispense

48

with any of the legitimate devices, no doubt comes from a misconception of the precise potentialities of these artifices. It is true, if they do not serve as a means to an end; an integral part of the play; units in the development of the story; then they not only may, but should, be dispensed with, by all means. We employ nothing—property, actor, scene, spectacle, spoken word, insert, incident or device—in the perfect photoplay that has not a bearing on the climax of the play.

The caption—variously miscalled leader, sub-title, etc.—is the most necessary, the most difficult and the most powerful of the illusory agents employed in screening the dramatic story. Its importance to the writer may be reckoned from the fact that it is one of the few small parts of the photoplay that is supplied by the author and shown intact to the audience. The caption is an action-title and, like the chapter headings of a novel, portions and savors the great bulk of the story and collectively gives its gist.

(EXAMPLE 10.) Take, for instance, the captions of "The Coming of the Real Prince" (Reliance), and we have the big moments in the play that made

49

it impossible for the audience to lose its vital significance: (1) ANNIE'S WIDOWED MOTHER, LEFT PENNILESS, OPENS A BOARDING HOUSE; (2) THE DRUDGE; (3) ANNIE FINDS SOLACE IN "CINDERELLA"; (4) THE DREAM OF PRINCE CHARMING AND THE WONDROUS CITY BEGINS; (5) "NO, BUD, I HAVE GIVEN MY HEART TO A WONDERFUL PRINCE;" (6) THE COMING OF THE PRINCE; (7) THE FOLLOWING SUNDAY THEY GO FOR A STROLL IN THE ENCHANTED FOREST; (8) THE FAIRY TREASURE—HIDDEN BY ANNIE'S MISERLY FATHER; (9) THE PRINCE SEES AN EASY OPPORTUNITY TO FILCH TWO TREASURES; (10) THE FLIGHT TO THE WONDROUS CITY OF DREAMS; (11) THE MAGIC AWAKENING OF MOTHER-LOVE; (12) "FOR THE PRINCE WAS A MIGHTY GOOD FELLOW!" (13) THE GLORY OF THE PRINCE'S DOMAIN BEGINS TO FADE; (14) "YOU WOULDN'T HAVE ME, MOTHER, SO I DREAMED OF A PRINCE!" (15) THE COMING OF THE REAL PRINCE ... And there's the complete story, which any one with imagination can readily fill out.

A play screened without captions or inserts would be wanting in all the little human, intimate and sympathetic touches that warm the heart and pitch the emotions of the audience. The figures that flitted thru the play, unintroduced, would be identified by the spectator as this or that actor, and not as Tess, or Mr. Barnes, or Sherlock Holmes—all *characters* of delightful memory. Pantomime sufficiently powerful to suggest every relationship; costume and accompaniments obvious enough to establish every environment; and action violent enough to interpret every emotion without the aid of captioned or inserted matter, belong to the elemental days of photodrama.

First of all, the caption should never be employed to tell of an action that is to follow in the scene, for a caption should never be used if it is possible to translate its essence into action:

(EXAMPLE 11.) For instance, in the following scene: Scene 56. JEWEL ROOM—Douglas has just finished forcing open the door of the jewel cabinet and holds the necklace in his trembling hand . . . it would have been superfluous to have captioned, DOUGLAS STEALS THE NECKLACE.

Too often important points are unsuccessfully left to the imagination of the audience because they have been so clear in the mind of the writer. Frequently these points are essential to preserve an unbroken continuity, yet too subtle to be conveyed by action, de-

51

109082

duction, suggestion, inference, implication or relationships.

(EXAMPLE 12.) *(a) To economize, by getting right into the pith of the story: ANNIE'S WID-OWED MOTHER, LEFT PENNILESS, OPENS A BOARDING HOUSE . . . introduces us to Annie and her mother, tells that her father has died, they are penniless, they must work, the place we find them in later is their boarding house. (b) To indi-cate a lapse of time and tell what worth-while has happened: THE SPRING COMES—AND WITH IT HER PRINCE . . . the previous scene had been in the winter, Annie has been dreaming of her prince and we might not have identified the weak, flashy young man as such; the caption is, also, a link in the suspense. (c) To communicate a mental or psychological process: THE DREAM OF PRINCE CHARMING AND THE WONDROUS CITY BEGINS. . . . contains the very essence of the climax and reveals the psychological trend of the entire play.*

We must bear in mind that there is some-thing more important than sequence of visible action, and that is unbroken continuity or per-fect cohesion of story unity—of which every intelligent audience is ever conscious—that knows no such thing as gaps, breaks or retrogressive movement. The caption is the bridge that spans these and supports, quickens and gratifies the imagination in addition.

The caption can be made to fulfill its most artistic function by combining all the essential qualities, already referred to, and also by serving as the action-title for a complete sequence of dramatic action. Thus one caption may cover all the scenes in a sequence, each caption adding a link in the development of the story and all together giving the gist of the story itself (as illustrated by Example 10). Thus the caption becomes a distinctive aid in building the dramatic plot, a contributory force in its expression, and a gratifying parallel to lead, guide and fulfill the action for the audience. Captions are not labels, but means of suggesting beyond the visible action and of furnishing deeper motives than those on the surface. There are beauty and harmony captions which often add a poetic touch, or an emotional tone, and intensify the dramatic effect.

(EXAMPLE 13.) THE FLIGHT TO THE WONDROUS CITY OF DREAMS . . . but we must take care that the poetic title is not a part of the harshly realistic play, for we are seeking integral

53

harmony. For example, in HELL—SECOND-HAND, we find captions to suit the theme: 10 MIN-UTES THIS SIDE OF ETERNITY! . . . THE LIFE-BLOOD RED FLAG.

An insert is filmed matter which is inserted in the appropriate place in a scene, the film being cut for this purpose. This matter must appear and be known as an insert to the writer and manufacturer only; to the audience, it becomes the normal, logical and only natural phenomena that could be presented under the circumstances and sustains and strengthens the illusion of reality. From the point of view of the screen, an "insert" would suggest something stuck in, or a patch; therefore it must never be recognized as such except in the workshop. Technically speaking, all inserted matter is inserts. From a mechanical point of view, the film must be cut in order that captions, printed or inscribed matter, close-views, visions, spoken lines, etc., may be inserted. But we should ignore the manufacturer's construction and consider inserted matter only as an essential to the perfect visualization of our dramatic story.

The letter, telegram and newspaper insert

54

are dangerous expedients to employ too frequently in the artistic photoplay. They are so easy to stick into a play that, like slang, they become a ready makeshift for the lazy mind, with results that are damaging to dignity.

We cannot repeat too often that everything employed in the photoplay is done so with a specific purpose, for a progressive effect, and for no other reason. Likewise, it must bear some cumulative and contributory relation to the climax. Thus inserts and captions must be something more than mere explanatory matter by becoming important contributory data.

The insert is a great factor for economy, and when properly used in this respect may contribute to heightened effects thru suggestive condensation.

(EXAMPLE 14.)   The following letter insert not only saves many scenes but teems with revelation: "Dearest—You simply cant stand it any longer. Come with me to the city at daybreak. Meet me in the office."   What it has told fills the gap; what it promises because of this audacious proposal makes the play.

The telegram is similar in character, only it allows still greater condensation:

(EXAMPLE 15). "Meet me in the office at daybreak." It serves as a further amplification of the same example, tho there is an obvious inconsistency in conveying such startling intelligence by wire.

The employment of the newspaper heading and paragraph is a decided novelty in conveying artistic data. The seeming awkwardness of the medium must be overshadowed by a simple and convincing naturalness on the part of the character in obtaining information from this source that strengthens its plea as dramatic material:

(EXAMPLE 16.) LIBRARY—Nelson enters with tray containing letters and papers. Shelburne opens paper, reads, pauses, laughs:
INSERT O . . . (News item heading)
  WEALTHY SOCIETY WOMAN LEARNS
    SHE HAS MARRIED BOGUS BARON
  Scene (Continued)
Shelburne thoughtful. Mary steals in and places her hand over his eyes. The fact disclosed in the item wiped out all the past that stood between Mary and Shelburne. The library scene was made more natural by the reading of the paper and what followed was inevitable. Neither the sense of the scene nor any conceivable action alone could have told adequately what really transpired. An insert alone filled the purpose.

Perhaps the most effective use of the insert

is to establish the premise of the plot, to cover the causes leading up to the opening of the play and possibly the relationship of the characters:

(EXAMPLE 17.) "Dear George:—As I write this I am preparing to run off with the Baron Komiskey. To be frank, I've gotten tired of not seeing you take any interest in anything. Forgive your former fiancée,
PETRONELLA."
In which we see the characters of both Petronella and George laid bare, besides furnishing a motive for George's change of character and future actions. This insert breaks the first scene.

The theory of breaking scenes with inserts has been discussed and has grounds for objections from an optical point of view only. The argument advanced against their use is based on the persistence of vision with which the eye retains for a considerable period the image of that which has passed before it, obscuring that which follows. This theory would become seriously operative when applied to inserts should we look upon them as extraneous matter—as for example the vaudeville acts that intervene between the parts of the long photoplays produced in many of the variety theaters. But, far from it, the ideal insert is

57

contributory dramatic material that rather precludes a possibility of gaps, jumps or discontinuity of dramatic sequence. The perfect insert emphasizes an otherwise too modest period of action. Optical delusion is a negligible quantity in the face of dramatic illusion, which sweeps everything mechanical before it.

To speak of inserts as *explanatory matter* is objectionable, because of the natural inference that the story is to be interrupted and the audience button-holed while a formal explanation is inserted. Unless an insert becomes essential· *interpretive material,* quickening the movement of the play and heightening the interest in the story, something must be wrong with the construction. Inserts should be classed with all other forms of essential interpretive material, such as expressive action, gestures and attitudes; logical characters and effective settings; and should be mercilessly dispensed with unless they fulfill a specific mission in carrying the story forward toward an inevitable climax.

The term, close-view, makes a finer distinction, signifying that an object or a portion of it is magnified, or that a close-view of a segment of the action is seen on the screen at close range by itself.

(EXAMPLE 18.) " . . . . *Annie reads letter, a great joy breaking over her face: INSERT LETTER. . . . "Dearest—Come with me to the city at daybreak."*

In which the letter is presented for our perusal with the same care that it would be inserted in a story at the proper moment. It is part of the story.

In the same manner a calling card, an inscription on a grave-stone, a monogram on a ring, a miniature photograph, may be brought, as it were, close to our eyes. The illusion is ingeniously preserved by the presence of the character's trembling or tracing fingers following the emotion in his soul.

The close-view, however, may take a step farther than merely photographing an inanimate object; it may dramatically emphasize a segment of exquisite action.

(EXAMPLE 19.) INSERT CLOSE-VIEW of title page of "Cinderella," Annie's trembling hand tracing first word . . . . INSERT CLOSE-VIEW of Annie's face, she closes her eyes, her lips move with a smile of ecstasy.

The close-view is indispensable for acute emphasis; for peculiar dramatic effect; for discernment of some essential object too small to be sufficiently noted or noticed otherwise; for the display of the finer and more subtle emotions; for the revealment of some otherwise hidden object or action important in unfolding the scene and developing the action. The last named takes the same latitude as fiction in bringing in essential data beyond the discernment of the human eye. The optical process, too, of looking at distant objects thru a strong glass is effectively reproduced by the close-view. A rather bizarre use is made of the same device by showing a sectional view of some inclosure:

(EXAMPLE 20.) The hero may be eavesdropping on the villain and be concealed in a box or a barrel; this fact is disclosed by means of the sectional view. Or a man crawling thru a tunnel and shaking the earth beneath the scene of action.

The close-view has no equal for breaking dangerously long scenes in a manner so natural and potential that oftentimes it makes a brilliant presentation of something that would in all probability have become tedious.

The vision insert is treated more particularly later on, under other captions. Suffice it to say, that the vision insert simulates the more subtle mental processes of thought and fantasy — such as reflection, introspection, dreams and hallucination—that have a simultaneous dramatic bearing on the conduct of the character and on the psychological development of the story.

(EXAMPLE 21.) CAPTION . . . . AFTER FIVE YEARS WITHOUT HER.
Scene 31. Simply marked grave in cemetery.
Malcolm discovered kneeling, closes his eyes. Fade to
INSERT VISION . . . . Reproducing scene 20 in part (great rock above beach, etc.). Fade to
INSERT VISION CLOSE-VIEW . . . . Malcolm looking intently at Florence, whose eyes disclose her tender love for him. Fade to
Scene 31 (Continued) Malcolm has opened his eyes, arms opened as tho to take Florence.

A helpful distinction between the simple insert and the close-view insert—tho they are both close-views, as a matter of fact—is to designate all static and inanimate matter that is neither alive nor in motion, as simple inserts; and that which is properly part of the action and has life, motion and expression, as close-view inserts.

61

*(EXAMPLE 22.)   Letters, telegrams, news ex-
cerpts, printed, carved, engraved matter, miniatures
or other likenesses reproduced, and objects incapable
of automatic effort are simply inserts. Close-views
of a hand, face, or other part of the anatomy under
the stress of emotion, or merely revealing a contributive peculiarity, remote objects with their con-
tingent action brought near, and fragments of action
isolated for emphasis, are close-view inserts.*

The question of the employment of dialog
at all in the photodrama has been widely discussed. It would seem to hinge on the meaning of the word "dialog." If the word is used
in its strict sense of "a conversation between
two or more persons," then we may eliminate
it from the photoplay without further question. The photoplay is no place for conver-
sations. But there are occasions upon which
the apt employment of a spoken line of dialog
has no equivalent or substitute. It becomes
one of the fine contributory elements that
establishes and preserves the illusion. The
effective use of the spoken line is usually as
an insert, being timed to appear simultaneously with the representation of its utterance:

*(EXAMPLE 23.)   To be precise, the insert follows
its actual utterance:*

Scene 23. Vine-covered arbor.
Follows business both pathetic and ludicrous of
Budd proposing: Annie smiles, shakes head.
INSERT SPOKEN LINE . . . . "NO, BUD, I
HAVE ALREADY GIVEN MY HEART TO A
WONDERFUL PRINCE!"
Scene 23. (Continued) Bud broken up but manly.

The spoken line is occasionally used also as
a caption, giving voice to the climacteric senti-
ment or situation in a single scene, or series
of scenes, that follows:

(EXAMPLE 24.) CAPTION 6 . . . . "TO BE
HANGED BY THE NECK UNTIL DEAD!" is
followed by a courtroom scene. The nature of the
proceeding is obvious. The judge rises and pro-
nounces the conventional sentence of death that gives
dramatic significance to the entire sequence of action
that follows.

The spoken line has a poignant directness
in it that is scarcely equaled by any other
piece of business. The mental process should
be so cunningly imitated that the enthralled
spectator hears the words he craved just as
distinctly as tho they had beat upon the drums
of his ears instead of the drums of his soul.
The words pierce the spectator with personal
sympathy, or antagonism, and fairly thunder

thru the silence. Like all other inserted matter and devices, the spoken line must not be used if it can be dispensed with to the artistic betterment of the play. It must come naturally and bridge a possible gap. It must be used as a supplement to, not a substitute for, effective action. Visualized action takes first and foremost place in the photoplay; all other matters are harmonious trappings and devices or illusion that decorate creaking mechanics with esthetic realities.

Inserted matter, unless artistically used, becomes theatric instead of dramatic. It becomes a sign of weakness and appears in the same light as clumsy explanations in stories written by inexperienced writers. The perfect photoplay leaves no doubts, offers no explanations, starts nothing it can not finish—it is all action, *action*, ACTION! And by action we mean technically visualized interpretation of whatsoever nature that convincingly contributes to the perfect illusion of emotionally seeing a dramatic story.

Visualization consists in giving tangible form to Inspiration; clothing Thoughts in flesh; creating living matter from Ideas; transmuting Emotions into thrilling substance; and peopling the imaginations of millions with the glorious company of Dreams come true, Desire gratified, Justice fulfilled, Brotherhood universal and Love triumphant!

CHAPTER V

VISUALIZATION

ITS RELATION TO ACTION; IMPORTANCE OF VOCABULARY; LITERATURE; TO REGISTER; INTERPRETATION; IN TERMS OF EMOTION; THE PART OF IMAGINATION

TECHNIQUE and rules, idea and action are as chaff on the threshing floor of the photodrama compared to visualization, which is the precious kernel to be sought. Visualization is both the key and the keynote of all photoplay-writing.

Hitherto, too much emphasis has been laid

65

on the importance of action, with but a half-formed idea of the true technical definition of the term, which is "the connected series of events upon which a piece depends; the main subject or story, as distinguished from an incidental action or episode." Too often has the novice had in mind the violent, whirling, feverish and physical action, familiarized by the "going into action" of the battlefield. Such action is always dynamic and spectacular, but not necessarily dramatic or interpretive. Everything is on the surface. It is all a matter of primal passion and primeval emotion. It is the stuff that melodramas are made of. But the deeper, more powerful and moving emotions of a civilized people are not surfacial. Their true interpretation is not expressible in immediate violent action. Culture and civilization are recognized and realized thru their repression of passion. Even the savage and the dumb beast have their refined emotions, expressed most vividly thru unwonted inertness or carefully concealed cunning.

(EXAMPLE 25.) The eternal mother-heart broods in dark corners over its dead offspring; it

66

softly croons over and gently caresses its babe;
deepest hate is manifested by the savage or sage
thru cunning, soft-footed revenge and veiled thrust.

There are two sides to the technical difficulties that confront the photoplaywright.
Given the conception of an idea worth while,
he must first have the power to visualize its
phenomena to himself; he must then be able
to represent its dramatic development visibly
in terms of action and symbols of emotion.
The power to visualize a story to one's self
can neither be taught nor learned; its exercise
lies in the gift of imagination. The ability to
represent this story in a form that may be
readily interpreted depends on a practical as-
similation and a working knowledge of dramatic construction and photoplay technique.
It resolves itself into the task of telling the
story indirectly with "business," instead of by
direct discourse.

A careful examination of the conditions of
photoplay acceptance has revealed a curious
and valuable piece of information. An unusu-
ally large percentage of the manuscripts received by producing companies contain good
ideas, but they are very often rendered

unacceptable because of imperfect and unilluminating expression. The editor, the director and the actor must understand from your scenario *exactly* what action, interpretation and suggestion your words are intended to convey. Many big ideas, striking situations and splendid scenes never see the light of the screen because of the photoplaywright's poverty of expression.

A broad vocabulary hesitates at no flight of inspiration, no matter how transcending; it falters at no wave of emotion, no matter how profound; it pauses at no thought, no matter how beautiful. "Beyond words," "inexpressible" and "indescribable" are confessions of literary and dramatic weakness that disappoint editors and bring manuscripts back by return mail. There are human words to express every impression that the human mind records. The language of the heart, of the soul and of the photoplay is the language of the dictionary. Familiarity with words begets fluency and accuracy in their use. There is but one word to express one situation under a given condition; do not be content until you find it. That diligence alone will make the finished and suc-

68

cessful writer. Given inspiration, the right words to express it will carry it to production, perhaps fame.

Perfect visualization, then, demands an exquisite command of language capable of nicely interpreting the finest shades of pathos, the deepest wells of passion, the most delicate waves of emotion, and a thousand grades of feeling.

Passing from the literary construction of the manuscript and play, we must become familiar with the mode of translating ideas, which must be clearly indicated by the writer. The three possible modes are by means of psychological action, suggestive attitude and mimetic expression. These are the elements of the new mimetic art of the photodrama just as the notes and keys are to music; words and sentences to literature; pigments and brushes to painting.

The secret of visualization lies in the nice employment of symbols of emotion. The danger lies in over-emphasis, which the writer can forestall by using an indirect or relative method, which means a constant exercise of repression.

(EXAMPLE 26.)   A girl is made to show pity for a sister-woman who is weeping because of some fell blow.   She does not go over and embrace her; that would show sympathy and participation.   Pity comes into her face, her poise of the head, her wistful attitude.   And if sympathy, she would probably stand with hand half-raised in helplessness if the woman was bereaved.   If some lighter grief, she would gently caress the other and smile encouragement.   Gentleness is poignant!

It is the thoughtful addition of the little human touches and scenes that makes the great plays and gives appropriate expression to great ideas.

(EXAMPLE 27.)   In scene 8, of "The Coming of the Real Prince," we see Annie being driven from the kitchen by her unfeeling mother.   The gist of the story would have been clear without dilating on this sequence.   But the tragedy in Annie's heart that was responsible for the play needed further visualizing, so we see Annie passing up the back stairs with a broken-hearted look in her eyes; we see her cast herself upon her miserable cot and sob as tho her heart would break.

(EXAMPLE 28.)   In scene 22, of the same play, we see the very depths of Annie's soul visualized. First in the caption: THE DREAM OF PRINCE CHARMING AND THE WONDROUS CITY BEGINS.   Annie, in grotesque position in bed

beside battered lamp, reading "Cinderella." Close-view shows her face, with lips moving, anecstatic smile lightening her features. We return to the scene and see the book slip from her fingers, and in her dreaming sleep her hands clasp on her breast; she raises her hand as tho she saw someone approaching. A vision-scene pictures Prince Charming in doublet and hose. Returning to the scene again we find Annie wakened, with her hand over her eyes as tho what she saw was too brilliant to look upon.

The photoplay is silent only technically. In order that convincing illusion be accomplished, there must be a successful registration of all such sounds as affect the characters and action in the normal and natural development of the play. We are interested only in such sounds as have a direct bearing on the matter that holds the attention of the audience. In other words, it must—like all other interpretive matter—be *contributory.*

In indicating that the character hears a particular sound, we say that he "registers" it. The term register has been used too generally in photoplay construction to indicate what actors shall do under the stress of every emotion.

71

(EXAMPLE 29.) For instance, "Annie registers anger," or "hate," "that she will not consent to something," "that she is displeased." A character who registers anything taking place in his own heart or soul becomes merely an actor—he is pretending. Characters do not pretend—they ARE. They do not register their feelings—they FEEL them with results unquestionably natural.

Sounds are recorded then thru reflex action, or registration, just as they actually reflect against the drums of the ear, telling the hearer that vibrations have been produced affecting the ear. Sounds are visualized by showing the appropriate affect on the character or characters.

(EXAMPLE 30.) We might have a deaf old father and his daughter. Her forbidden lover is behind a stone wall. He whispers softly several times before she is conscious of his call. She turns, joyously, and the two pantomime behind the old man's back.

Sounds are even more effectively visualized thru the employment of one or more correlative scenes.

(EXAMPLE 31.) In one case we see someone in the act of calling; in the next we see the call registered. The intervening distance may be gauged by the amount of energy expended by the character.

72

Or we may see a man escaping from peril, he stumbles and falls. The next scene shows the captors registering the noise of his fall.

In the elemental days of the cinematograph, it seemed improbable that music could ever be effectively registered. The visualization of strains of music, however, has met with most successful accomplishment. It is effected thru a careful imitation of the auricular and mental process of recording sound, combined with the use of symbols of emotion.

(EXAMPLE 32.) "The Lost Melody" (Vitagraph) is a play the plot of which is based on visualized sound. A strain of music sung and heard by a man under most virtuous circumstances is repeated when he is on the point of committing a crime, and it saves his soul. . . . In one scene we see the four leading characters walking along and singing each his love song, with his soul in his face; next we see the dancers at the club pausing and listening, some of the rapture of the singers faintly transmitted to their faces; in the roadway an automobile party stops, they put their hands behind their ears and listen, two keeping time, the other two put the spirit of the song in action and steal a lover's kiss.

(EXAMPLE 33.) Five years later the song is sung to save Douglas. The mental process of receptivity is imitated. We see Malcolm on the terrace singing; a close-view is then screened of a line

73

of the music and words; then we see Douglas paus-
ing in his act of robbing his best friend, registering
in alarm; then what he suddenly sees in his mind
and heart is visioned, being the scene of that wonder-
ful night years ago.

Thus the silent drama may become vibrant
with emotional music and resonant with
tongues that need no interpreter, for all na-
tions understand the universal language of the
heart. The most sublime characters and val-
iant deeds, ravishing color and mellifluous
voices, are in our soul; sublime sympathy is
in our world-old heart; profound understanding is in our God-given reason, and this multi-
glorious human marvel is gratified to the ut-
most in having its humanity called into active
being.

The leading characters must become the center of all action; the supernumeraries are nothing more or less than animated portions of the set itself.

CHAPTER VI

Characterization

IDENTITY AND PERSONALITY; CHARACTERISTICS AND IDIOSYNCRASIES; DESCRIPTION AND DELINEATION; ESTABLISHING RELATIONSHIP; MOTIVES; EXPRESSION; CONTRASTS.

IF we will view characters and characterization as elements of interpretive and contributory matter, along with inserts, setting and action, it should aid us in building perfect climaxes. This view would protect us from that error resulting from the leading characters seizing the bit in their teeth, so to speak, and running amuck with the story. Characters are subservient to climax. We have no use for any manifestations of their character outside of the needs of properly developing the big

75

moment of the story. Character is the most effective means to our photoplay end.

Photoplay actors in particular should become exquisite interpreters of character. Directors should be skillful managers and directors of interpretation and other mechanical detail. The photoplaywright alone should be the originator and creator of ideas and an expert in their expression. But, because photoplaywriting has been in a crude elemental state, and the new mimetic art of photoplayacting has had to be slowly and thoughtfully developed, abuses have crept in. Too often the director becomes the self-appointed creator, interpreter and adapter, withholding complete knowledge of the play from the actors and remaking the author's artistic ideas according to the mold of his own mental and emotional understanding, and the mechanical and material equipment he has at his command, or deems essential. Still, we cannot too harshly blame the officious director until the photoplaywright has become an indubitable master of expressive and comprehensive "business."

Photodrama differs radically from the short

story, in that there are at least two leading characters, instead of a single predominating, all-absorbing character. Such a character would be capable of little else than the development of itself thru introspection, reminiscence and possibly ambition, which would result in a character study. A character study is next to impossible in photodrama. An internal struggle of one being with himself can sustain but a few scenes at most. There must be two, or more, souls (and bodies) struggling to accomplish, overthrow or maintain a certain end.

We find in the photoplay, then, two leads, or leading characters, at least; while there may be often three or four. All the important action surrounds these characters. We see the characters in their characterizations standing out clearly as symbols of the motives and forces in the play. The hero and the heroine battle for, and accomplish, the gratifying conclusion; the villain and his accomplices employ their villainous designs in an unprincipled effort to overthrow the good, wholesome and happy elements. Obstacles thrown in the path of one side constitute suspense, and in their removal form a situation.

77

After the leads, there may be an economical number of supernumeraries to carry the action along with logical environment and natural life-likeness.

(EXAMPLE 34.) A courtroom, a busy street, the floor of the stock exchange, or any other setting wherein other characters should appear to naturalize it, must be appropriately peopled. These characters are animated portions of setting and contribute to harmony.

The early identity, or differentiation between the leads themselves, and between the minor characters is of vast moment and importance. The moment a character appears, or is discovered in a scene, his identity must be disclosed, and his relationship to the other characters and the action made known.

There are three ways of establishing identity: (a) thru personality, which discloses strength or weakness of character and the manner in which it dominates or is subservient to others with whom it comes in contact; (b) by means of idiosyncrasies, or marked personal oddities, deformities, or deportment; (c) vocational garb, national characteristics, uniform or peculiarity of personal ensemble.

78

CHARACTERIZATION

(EXAMPLE 35.) *(a) The line, "Mother weeping and Annie supporting her," in Scene 1 of "The Coming of the Real Prince," foretells a certain strength and weakness that manifests itself thru the two characters. (b) A character exhibits a continual frown, or sniffs, or winks, or limps, or has a scar or deformity. (c) As a soldier, policeman, a character would wear his uniform, or a foreigner might wear all or part of his native costume, etc.*

Strong personalities flourish in the serious drama, while the leads in comedy are usually distinguished by peculiarities. Each human being has his normal characteristics that differentiate him from the rest of his fellows; this must become well marked in photodrama, tho not exaggerated to the point of becoming a personal oddity. They must be clearly brought out and maintained in a dignified manner thruout the play. In the serious play, character is but a means of developing a moving *personality,* and personality is but the outward symbol of the internal truths of the story. Personality is motive visualized.

Your few words describing your characters and indicating their actions must be suggestive enough to enable the combined efforts of director and actor to delineate truthfully the personality that is part of your dramatic vision. Nothing stands still in the photoplay; therefore characters must be delineated in terms of emotion—repressed or active—or described in words of action—commonplace or dramatic. The audience should be informed unimstakably who and what your characters are *thru what they do*. The motives of the leading characters must come to the surface at once in order to ignite the audience's interest with the dramatic spark. There must be sufficient insinuation in *what* your characters do, to reveal *why* they do it. Altho a character, during the action of the play, may develop from weakness to strength, yet each bit of action has a determining character of its own, that is either weak or strong.

The immediate and unmistakable identity of your characters is essential to knowing your characters; the early and clear establishment of relationship between characters is essential to grasping your story. A profound study of the subject yields the conclusion that the simplest, most economical, quickest and most effective means of revealing the identity and establishing the relationship of the character is the caption. Without the caption we must resort to the inartistically obvious and more or less clumsy devices, such as doors labeled "Private Office of John Smith"; trade-signs, as "Solomon Isaacs, Pawnbroker," or have the actors overgesture their parts in a laborious effort to tell the audience who and what they are.

(EXAMPLE 36.) A perusal of six produced plays discloses the unanimous use of the caption for the combined purposes of identity and relationship. These captions usually appear early in the play— before the second or third scene: (1) GEORGIA WANTS TO BE A LEADER OF HER SEX AND NOT A DRUDGE; (2) ANNIE'S WIDOWED MOTHER LEFT PENNILESS; (3) COLONEL FARRINGTON FORCES HIS DAUGHTER ON MARSTON, HIS SUPPOSED BENEFACTOR; (4) MALCOLM DECIDES TO WAIT AND MAKE HIS PROPOSAL TO ROSALIE AN ARTISTIC OCCASION; (5) SHELBURNE, HARD HIT, TURNS AGAINST HIS IRRE-SPONSIBLE LIFE; (6) ARCHER DURAND AND HIS WIFE ARRIVE IN THE MINING DISTRICT HALF STARVED.

The letter insert can be employed with equal effectiveness. The characters once introduced effectively, their future actions are easily understood—providing they are logical

81

and natural. The relationships, as they are established by the first appearances of the characters, form the premise of the plot and the argument of the story that are readily followed, if the scenes are well-knit and the story interesting.

In conjunction with the caption or letter, then, something occurs immediately to grasp the attention and offer insight into characters, their relationships and motives. Furthermore, both vocation and character may be indicated by environment, make-up, costume, tools, manner and culture. Contrasts in action, appearance and conduct between characters is always effective in clarifying characterization. Where there are no voices and many characters, great care must be exercised to differentiate. The sooner the writer realizes the difficulties that beset actor and director in differentiating character, the quicker he will begin to economize on the number he employs and to strengthen personalities. It is an axiom of photodrama that the bigger the idea, *the fewer the characters!* Thus it is seen that too many important characters make too great a demand on the audience.

In order that the character may exhibit the motive underlying the action, the writer must visualize it, and the actor must realize it. There must be mimetic harmony, sympathy and naturalness.

We are cautioned by some savants never to tell the actor *how* to act a line, but tell them only *what* to do. We disagree. Providing the writer has become an expert in the writing of business and dramatic expression, he can scarcely infringe on the director's right, the actor's profession, or injure the prospects of his play by offering an analysis of the construction of the characters he himself has created. Co-operation is too often lacking from the fact that the actor seldom knows exactly what he is trying to do. The director extricates a jumbled part from the inseparable whole of the play, recites it extempore for the actor and drills the requisite action into him. How, then, can the actor be expected to interpret things and put them in that were in the mind of the writer? He must guess at the harmony of the composition, surmise the relationships, and consequently lose all the nice touches that the true artist would incorporate

83

in the well-made play. It is the actor's sole
business and art to interpret ideas. He is the
living motive of the play and the most important symbol in the expression of its inner
truth. When will actors learn their lines in
order to catch the very soul of your play, instead of yah-yahing at each other when a
visualized exchange of words is necessary?
But the writer will have to write the essential
words—perhaps that's the rub?

Violent action will always excite and thrill
the mind; but it takes passive repression to
move the soul. The body that suffers, writhes
and flings itself about; the hurt soul shrinks
back and lies stunned. The prick of a pin will
make a strong man jump spasmodically a foot
in the air; a sharp word will make the noblest
soul sink deep into gloom. We actors, directors and playwrights are seeking the artistic
expression of the life of the soul; the existence
and agency of the body are merely means to
that end. We should be striving to capture
the soft lights and shadows of mental impres-
sionism; and not be struggling to imprison
the bold sunlight and harsh lines of physical
photography. Deep emotion and its character-

ization lies not in the bold step forward, but in the shrinking half-step backward; not in the brazen eye, but in the shy, drooping eye-lid; not in the defiant word, but in the silent, quivering lip; not in the blow of the fist, but in the gentle, stroking hand; not in the violent embrace, but in the tender caress; not in the sudden turn on the heel, but in the shrug of the shoulders—one is a matter of physical mechanics, the other emotional art. If emotional art is put first in our endeavors, all the range of physical mechanics will follow logically, but secondarily.

Our writers have been frightened away from suggestive artistic detail, and have fallen upon the evil way of bald physical mechanics that leave nothing to the imagination. The gentle gesture, the poise of the head, the trembling lip, the downcast eye, of the story vision are usurped by the over-emphasized action. Decisive action is essential in the photoplay, but the producer's version is too often another story.

Characters should tend to personify and visualize the tender twilights of pathos; the soft shadows of pain and sorrow; the gentle glow of goodness and nobility; the serene surface of happiness. They should build the lives of the audience anew; inspire them to noble deeds; let them touch the hem of the garment of sublimity and teach them life's lessons of humility, forbearance and faith.

The playwright should never take advantage of his audience's moral weakness to display "strong" scenes of character depravity; but rather he should employ a character's weakness to strengthen his audience's morality.

CHAPTER VII

THEME, TREATMENT AND THE CENSOR

MORALS AND ETHICS; CRIME; NATIONAL BOARD OF CENSORSHIP; TASTE; INSPIRATION AND INFLUENCE.

WHAT shall we write about, and how shall we write it?

Here the playwright must pause and look his fellow men, his friends, his parents, his children, his wife, and his conscience square in the eye. They are one and all his intimate audience. They will be influenced by his product, be pleased or offended in its production, and thru it see his heart with all its strength and weakness laid bare.

Broadly, our theme shall be Life—Life in

all its aspects: the gorgeous and the threadbare; the noble and the sordid; the happy and the sorrowful; the righteous and the sinful; the healthy and the ailing; the youthful and the aged; the strong and the weak. But it must be the *life that we know*—not necessarily thru experience, but possibly thru study, observation or intuition.

Choice of theme is a matter requiring, chiefly, a respectful observance of the general popular demand and the particular needs of the studios, unless you are genius enough to initiate and lead the popular tastes. But the subject of treatment is one requiring a far more delicate exercise of judgment. Any conceivable theme may be spoiled by an indiscreet or injudicious viewpoint.

The playwright conveys powerful personalities to his characters, but remains passively impersonal himself. He immovably records truth, never interposing himself, his opinions or his bias. His characters pursue their own lives; they are neither automatons nor marionettes; they live according to their individual natures and have provokingly free wills.

The photoplaywright has but to remain on

the side of right and justice, good citizenship and decency. He communicates nothing thru the symbols of his play that he would hesitate, refrain or be ashamed of telling those nearest, dearest and most sacred to him. Public audiences are daily made up of millions of people, who are highly impressionable, of tender age and of simple susceptibilities. Providing our play is effective, it contains a very positive influence, that means either a rise or a fall in moral values in every community wherein it is exhibited. The playwright must be the figure of justice that shows no mercy to the wrongdoer; the sword of retribution he carries in one hand, in the other he holds the scales of just rewards. There simply must be a moral ending.

It is more essential that the villain be vanquished, than punished. Our story is not vengeance, but is usually concerned with the victory of the good element—or hero—and the incidental adventures of circumventing the villain and misfortune. Stories in which the good element is overcome by the bad, thus placing a premium on the bad, are unmoral. Stories or plays showing the delights to be gained from illicit pleasures or pursuits, followed or not by adequate punishment or retribution, are immoral.

(EXAMPLE 37.) Thus the so-called "white slave," "drug terror" and underworld plays, reeking with depravity, leering with lasciviousness and groveling in intemperance, are actually immoral. Their symbols of vice are all-powerful, and any symbols of virtue introduced are usually wishy-washy in comparison. The hero or heroine is usually a weak character, instead of a strong one. We see vice exercising a baneful influence, robbing its victim of will, health and life. Vice conquers. We do not need "examples" of what not to do. We should be inspired by the nobility of good, and not cowed by the fear of evil. The countless throngs that crowd the exhibition of these so-called plays for the most part are craning to get a view of gleaming flesh quivering in pools of forbidden passion, rather than seeking a glimpse of a tortured soul—neither one being an edifying entertainment.

At first thought, it would seem as tho crime were the most frequent factor among the sources of dramatic construction. As a matter of fact, accomplished crime does figure powerfully in more than two-thirds of all dramatic productions, including the highest class. Active vice, the venial and deadly sins and potential crime occur even more frequently thruout the course of our dramatic development. It would seem as tho we should have no little difficulty in making our good characters walk the straight and narrow path among such a net work of pitfalls.

But even the writer of the most moral plays should glory in the omnipresence of sin and crime, tho never glorify it. Good would be colorless as dramatic material, were it not for evil. Evil is the foil for goodness; it is the contrast that delivers goodness from monotony; evil is the shadow that gives the highlight of goodness its chiaroscuro; it is the salt that saves it from saccharinity. When evil, misfortune, or bereavement oppose us, they oftentime bring to the surface and develop our otherwise hidden virtues, making them illuminate the lives of others and add a ray of undying nobility to the world's fiction experience.

(EXAMPLE 38.) Five produced plays selected at random reveal the following facts in relation to the employment of crime: (1) THE COMING OF THE REAL PRINCE—An immoral, flashy man of the city attempts to seduce an innocent, visionary country girl. He is thwarted by the rousing of dead mother-

*love and of a sublime nobility in a country yokel; (2)
THE LOST MELODY—The memory of his sweet,
innocent dead wife, brought back to him thru hearing
a forgotten melody, stays a man's hand from robbing
his best friend; (3) UNTO THE CHILDREN—A
boy inherits the vice of gambling from his father,
but it is burnt forever out of his nature, by the sublime heroism and sacrifice of his mother at the critical
moment; (4) THE STRUGGLE—The brutal assault
of strikers on a strike-breaker, brings the capitalist
and laborers face to face on a common plane of pity
and nobility; (5) BRANDED FOR LIFE—An ex-
convict, striving in vain for reinstatement in the
eyes of society, is enabled thru a noble and inspiring
sacrifice to win the respect of all men.*

A play will exert influence in the same pro-
portion as it is artistically effective; which is
as much as to say, the greater the artist the
greater his power for good or evil. To become
over-zealous in presenting morality leads to
propaganda; to be too realistic and careless
in the portrayal of immorality leads into the
mire of obscenity. True art has nothing to
do with morality, for or against; it is
intrinsically noble, uplifting and inspiring.
Whether the life of the artist is exemplary
or not is a matter of his own conscience; the
life of his character creations must keep with-

in the bounds of decency, be amenable to the laws of the country and subject to the rewards and punishments gratifying to the best impulses of the wholesome minded.

Tragedy is an exception, in that we often see a good character overwhelmed by circumstances, environment and nature. But tragedy should conform to inspiration, in that we behold the doomed character revealing unguessed sublimity in the unequal struggle.

Together with this question of treatment comes that of, "How real do we want our realism?" It is answered indirectly by saying that just so much of any of life's experiences as we may disclose or relate in promiscuous company, in the presence of innocent—not necessarily ˙ puritanic—understandings and quick perceptions, may be delineated on the screen. Each age has its own broadnesses and limitations in this respect, of which every refined and intelligent person is cognizant. Drama is not dependent upon frank discussions of revolting or lascivious subjects; entertainment is its prime function. A searching analysis of either vice or virtue is contrary to the principles of dramatic action.

The actual commission of crime is not as important as the cause and effect of it. Morbid curiosity is the only excuse for the sight of a deed of murder, suicide, or other vicious crime. *How* a crime is committed is an element of criminology, not drama.

We have to thank the National Board of Censorship for the exclusion of actual deeds of crime. This censoring body, unfortunately, has been composed almost wholly of persons who are theoretically the very antipodes of crime and naturally intolerant to its employment at all. Time may bring us a less biased exercise and a broader view of their powers.

(EXAMPLE 39.) Criminal deeds are easily and effectively handled in photoplay. For instance, murder—we see the culprit and the victim in separate scenes: a man at his desk in one scene; the murderer breaking into the office, in another. Another scene brings us to the instant BEFORE the deed—the weapon poised, or culprit and victim in mortal combat. We may here interpose a scene of someone registering a pistol shot, or hearing the scuffle. In another scene we return to the crime and find it has just been committed. Any crime may be effectively delineated in this manner.

In the matter of casting characters, no

character can properly be cast a villain unless his actions comprehend a conscious knowledge of guilt. Our hero oftentimes commits a crime or misdemeanor unwittingly, or in that stage of his character development before the elements of the story itself change him from weak to strong. The thoroly bad character must remain bad, just as he would in life; the good character may be bad temporarily and become bettered, but we must make him suffer from his misdeeds. In other words, our characters become *living people* who are endowed with human traits of which their every action is the natural outcome.

Good taste in the selection and treatment of theme brings us back again to the same admonition of exercising the simple quality of being well-bred. Just as we would not think of startling a drawing-room assembly by forcing our personal bias upon it, so we must select our dramatic matter in a serious, humane and delicate manner. There are potent commercial reasons, as well as the dogma of good taste, for not caricaturing races, ridiculing creeds, satirizing politics and making fun of physical deformities and mental infirmities.

Occasion, occupation and environment each has it own propriety and convention that must carefully be observed by the photoplaywright. This is not a matter of delicacy so much as it is one of producing conviction thru naturalness.

(EXAMPLE 40.) The seashore is an occasion for women wearing extremely abbreviated costumes that would be improper in the street; the occupation of the doctor is one that perm.its women to enter his quarters alone with propriety; the environment of the Orient makes it a convention for women to smoke and guests to sit on the floor.

In summing up this most important phase of the photodrama, we may say briefly: Let your sympathies ever be found with the purest, best and noblest there is in life; make your story show your condemnation of the low and evil. But don't be a prude or a preacher! Do not permit yourself to be accused of trying to teach better things, but let your work *inspire* them!

Technique is the Training School of all organized knowledge; Art is its Life: Technique is a matter of Rules and a space of study; Art is one of principles and eternity.

CHAPTER VIII

RULES OF THE GAME

DURATION AND NUMBER OF SCENES; PERPETUAL MOTION; THE "NOW" ELEMENT; EFFECTIVE FORM; NATURAL LAWS; SCENE PRINCIPLE.

IN no literary effort is technique more important or essential than in the construction of the photoplay. There are arbitrary rules that must be followed and conventions that cannot be ignored. We must cater to the manufacturer's possibilities; we must conform to fixed mechanical limitations; we interpret our art thru "business"; we must gather the world-wide vision within the narrow focus of the camera's eye. Our play-form and technique

97

must be sufficiently potent, suggestive and revealing to enable competent co-operators to discern, interpret and manufacture an effective concrete and vividly *alive* reproduction of our abstract vision, so that it may be readily recognized and emotionally realized by independent audiences the world over.

The photoplaywright is the only literary craftsman who does not carve, model and perfect with his own handiwork the actual presentment of his creation offered to the public. And, greatest obstacle of all—our photoplaywright must accomplish his eloquent task by remaining technically silent! We come to the inevitable conclusion that construction and technique are equal in importance—if not superior—to idea or conception of the writer.

The matter of bare photoplay form is but the slightest move in the direction of perfect effect. It is the subject of *effective* photoplay form and how to produce the effects that really count.

We may set down as one of the first principles of photodrama, that the playwright must make his rule of construction: People go to the theater to *see* a deed and not to read or

hear *about* it.   There are several ways of con-
struing a breach of this principle.   The first
is that of telling the story indirectly by means
of captions and inserts, instead of directly
thru consecutive action.   This is the method
of the poor plotter and shallow artificer who
sticks in a caption or insert whenever he en-
counters an obstacle, oftentimes skipping the
climacteric situations and showing the trifling
details.

*(EXAMPLE 41.)   AFTER THE RIOT JOE
KEPT IN BED WITH BROKEN ARM . . . . Audiences simply will not accept that broken arm as convincing unless their reasons can vouch for the violence
that led to it. But riots are more easily skipped than
successfully delineated.   All climacteric scenes must
be shown and not merely referred to.   We always
take the commonplace for granted; but never the
extraordinary.*

Next we deal with an offending heritage
from short story fiction, the story within a
story or, as we shall here call it, a story within
a play.   It should never be resorted to; it need
never be done.   It breaks the thread of one
story to insert another that in nearly every
case is stronger than the original, forming
an anti-climax instead of contributing to one.

99

Its use means that the play has not been carefully plotted, that it has not been begun early enough, or in the right place, and that it is trying laboriously to explain something that would not stand by itself.

(EXAMPLE 42.) In the Vitagraph's "A Million Bid," the quasi-hero is picked up again after having been absent for more than a reel, and sets in to tell what has happened to him while he has been away! Most of it was entirely "another story," but much of it might have been effectually interwoven with the progressing action of the play. As it was, it was most difficult to grasp the fact that we had been hauled months back in point of time. In the mental melée we lost sight of the main theme altogether, and most of us never quite got back to it. All of us were befuddled to some extent. It was intended, no doubt, that the audience should not know the identity of the narrator until the heroine herself found it out, which would have made it worse in thus having an entire stranger break into our story and consume nearly one-third of the entire play!

The most common form of a story within a play is the one in which the hunter, or the veteran, or the old person blighted in love, or some such character sits down, with a younger person usually, and in the end there is a laborious effort to make the experience of the older person play a part in the younger's career. There may be exceptions to a hard-and-fast rule of avoiding these devices, but usually it will be found that there is a remedy in the principles of the photodrama itself that say begin your action back at *the very beginning* and *always go forward.*

The third pitfall, is that of trying to record speeches—dramatic tho they be—by supposedly visualizing what the speaker is referring to; of trying to tell the story of a crime, for instance, thru the trial of the culprit, rather than by showing the events preceding and causing the trial in their chronological order. Here, as in the former instance, the vision is resorted to. The vision is apt to be employed in dramatizing the detective story that is primed with a surprise in the climax in which the method of its revealment is disclosed by going back and showing the steps. Let it be a rare exception that makes you ever turn backward; for neither time nor drama can do it without violating a natural law.

To be explicit, the photoplay is a *now* play! The now may be a thousand years ago, but it must be relived again, now. All of which should warn us to avoid long lapses of time, occurring especially in the one-part play.

Nothing quite emphasizes the "now" quality of the photodrama as the invariable practice of employing nothing but the *present tense* in writing the photoplay. Synopsis and scenario are seemingly conscious of the things they are engaged in doing now. Past deeds and future prophecies—employing their respective tenses —frequently occur in captions and inserts, however.

(EXAMPLE 43.) From a letter: "I have never seen you take any interest in anything." Caption: "In fifty minutes your child will be on the scrap heap, too!"

The laws of natural movement and action should never be violated by the characters themselves. Any character who is to appear in the next scene must always be seen to *leave* the present scene, disappearing from view in that action, and again be seen to *come on* the scene that follows. It is unnecessary to accompany the character thru the various and uninteresting steps between his leaving one scene and arrival on the next. If something dramatic happens to him en route then we should see it. Contrary to fiction construction, scene precedes character in presentation. We are carried to the new scene and meet the character at the door as it were, and the illusion is complete. A preliminary fragment of action transpiring in the following scene, before the appearance of the character, will lend a further contribution to naturalness.

(EXAMPLE 44.) *In scene 27, of "All Power for a Day," we find Alice hurriedly leaving the crowd when she has seen the face of the man she hates. In scene 28, the room in her boarding-house is shown, her landlady—her enemy's confederate—snooping for a bit among her things before she enters.*

Characters must not be left in one scene and be discovered in the next following. They are not clothing dummies or marionettes, to be picked up bodily and helplessly and placed in set poses for the inspection of the audience. If another scene intervenes in which the same character does not appear, then it is not necessary for him to "come and go," since we presume he has had time and freedom for the necessary action while we were engaged with the alternate scene.

The scene principle in the photoplay is one

of reflective power. One scene reacts, re-
bounds, reflects, reverberates from the scene
that precedes it to the scene that follows it;
all bear a cumulative relation toward the
climax.

*(EXAMPLE 45.) In "The Master of the Lost
Hills" we have six scenes all different, yet showing
the reflective power with tremendous force: (1)
Mary aims gun out of window and tells brother to
step back or she will shoot; (2) Brother hesitates in
his advance; (3) Close-view of Mary taking aim;
(4) Just at edge of woods Mary's desperate lover is
taking aim at her; (5) Portion of dense forest showing sheriff and posse, who have come to rescue Mary,
lost; (6) Exterior of shack shows mob drawing closer.*

Another scene principle that we have
learned is that every time the camera is shifted
an iota we have a new scene. Theoretically,
the eye of the camera never moves, excepting
in the disillusioning practice of some operators
to follow the movements of energetic characters by "panoram-ing."

Our rule for length, duration and number
of scenes is governed by the unalterable unit
of the reel, or 1,000 feet of film. A short play
—one reel—may consist of from 25 to 50
scenes; according to the directness, tone,

treatment by the author and the method of the director. The exciting play of comedy, adventure and peril moves along rapidly, with short, quick scenes and many "returns," just as in fiction we use short sentences and employ words and phraseology that remind us of and constantly revert to the hero's imminent peril. The duration of a scene is in direct ratio to the vital relationship of its action to the climax.

(EXAMPLE 46.) In "The Salt of Vengeance" the grief-crazed father of an injured child sets a bomb under the rails that will blow to atoms the child of the man who is responsible for the injury. The lunatic pens up the guilty man, taunts him with the swiftly approaching fate of his precious child. This scene endures for several minutes. The next is a mere "flash" of a speeding railroad train occupying several seconds.

It is a natural law of drama that demands the establishment of identity almost the moment that a character appears. This is especially requisite in photodrama because of the rapid panorama of scenes that hurry on and off, at the rate of 75 to 200 an hour. One moment's doubt on the part of the audience— so incredibly swift and fleeting is the hurry of photoplay events—may mean the misunderstanding or losing of a year of the hero's life.

Learn and follow rules always with a willing mind; but never let them lead you around by the nose. The man who cannot take a single step without consulting his rules will become a wooden worker. "The way to make rules really valuable is to thoroly learn them, then literally forget them by perfectly practicing them." Now and then we see something in a play that is superior to rules and technique; something that would have been cramped and crushed by rules. At present the photodrama has many superficial rules and a technique that is often archaic and lacks the element of futurity.

All said and done, we are not teaching technique, or laying down rules; rather, we are trying to interpret the laws of human conduct, the science of being natural and the art of entertaining effectively.

*Real success is not as likely to come
to the man who grinds out a play a
day, year in and year out, as it is to
him who writes "the play of the day"
once a year; film footage is not the
measure of photoplay fame.*

CHAPTER IX

Bromides Worth Repeating

THE VIRTUE OF ECONOMY; PRODUCING POLI-
CIES; PERIOD AND COSTUMES; ANIMALS;
COPYRIGHT AND CARBON COPIES; RELATION
OF AUTHOR'S WORK TO HIS AUDIENCE; TO
THE MANUFACTURER; TO HIS MANUSCRIPT.

SO many volumes have been written
merely *describing* the photoplay, repre-
senting it primarily as a *manufactured article*
and larding the treatises with an appalling
number of "dont's," that the author of
the present work has made an especial effort
constructively to analyze photodrama, to
embody it as a new and complete form of
drama-literary art, and show the student not

only what to do but *how to do it*. Hitherto, photoplay inception and construction have been carried on chiefly with a view to facilitating its manufacture. It is about time that we took the profit-yielding audiences into consideration by supplying the artistic entertainment for which they are crying. The manufacturing end is well able to take care of itself; the actor has demonstrated in a vast number of instances that he is able "to deliver the goods"—if he is supplied with them; a large number of directors have demonstrated remarkable ability in assembling and directing the material elements that perfectly interpret and visualize the story of the playwright. *All that is needed is the trained writer* in adequate numbers to supply the infinite demand. By the trained writer, is meant the man who needs the *artistic co-operation* of editor, director, actor and manufacturer, and not the mechanical collaboration with them.

It takes, then, a knowledge of the things that enable you to *do* your good idea effectively; a negligence of the don'ts will not make for the flawless play, yet alone would not succeed in smothering the great idea.

There are three relationships of the writer
that will bear repeated cautions and dont's:
(1) The Audience; (2) The Manufacturer—
(a) editor, (b) studio, (c) photography, (d)
manufacture; and (3) The Manuscript—(a)
technique, (b) preparation, (c) sale. We shall
discuss these considerations in the order
named.

1. THE AUDIENCE.—Your audience in
general is world-wide. Because of the brevity
of the plays, the cheapness of admission to
the theaters, and the quick and universal appeal to the emotions our first and most numer-
ous patrons are the lower classes and especially the children. For these reasons alone,
suggestiveness, the portrayal of crime in such
a way as to show how it is done, or as to
inspire its commission, are not to be exploited.
Taking sides with either the masses or the
classes; with labor or capital, or with the
white race versus races of color, is not only inartistic but dangerously incendiary. Politics
are too local as play material, as we must
always bear in mind that our play is to appear
in Timbuctoo as well as in Tonopah. Re-
ligion is too delicate, too cherished and too

sacred a subject for anything but dignified and unprejudiced treatment. Films that *in any way reflect* upon the Roman Catholic Church will be barred out of many Catholic countries. The European market is a most profitable source of income to many American manufacturers. In this connection we have but to remember that the human heart has the same strength and struggle, the same weaknesses and tragedies the world over. Difference of language, however, raises a few minor pitfalls. For example, placards of warning, ransom, rewards and other matter which play a part in the story thru the audience's reading it in the picture, should be eliminated. These points are easily circumscribed—and made more effective—by the use of the insert. Just as captions have to be made in the language of each exhibiting country, so do the proper inserts.

2. MANUFACTURER. (a) *Editor* — Some reader will have to pass on your manuscript, in all likelihood, before the editor sees it. In both cases, the Synopsis becomes the gate of approval. They do not read the Scenario at all unless the Synopsis is

eminently promising. An editor wants what he needs, rather than what he personally desires to see presented. Your manuscript might contain the most pleasing and producible play in the world, yet if it did not fit his existing needs it would be poor policy to purchase it. Your manuscript is its own appeal and needs no personal letter; it is advisable not to write one. Your title is surely going to influence the editor strongly for or against further perusal of the manuscript. The editor will naturally be partial to the short Synopsis, but do not coddle this partiality by making your Synopsis too bald. The editor does not accept a manuscript, as a rule, until he has held a conference over it—possibly with the managing-director of the company adapted to producing the type of story in question. A careful observance of the rule of economy—economy of supers and principals, of *interior sets,* of props, of difficult scenes, of energy, time and expense—is bound to be appreciated.

(b) *Studio*—In the term studio, we may include director, actor, stage carpenter, and interior lightings and effects. No one is more pleased with a simple and powerful story than the director, and frequently no one has quite as much to say about the acceptance of the manuscript as this same highest-paid employee. It has often happened that even a bought manuscript of undoubted merit has never seen the light of the screen because there have been several difficult scenes to master, either mechanically or emotionally. The manuscript must be concise and quick in showing the director how many sets must be constructed or got out, how many actors must be employed, what props and costumes must be bought, rented or ordered. It is in this relation, that a scene plot may be used to advantage, for it will enable the director to consider the matter of suitable locations for exteriors. Unless he has child actors available, the matter of juvenile leads may mean the rejection of an otherwise desirable play. Military, costume or period plays are sure to be frowned down unless it is the producing policy of the manufacturer to put them on. Unless the producer has at his command trained animals, either wild or tame, it will be a waste of postage to send him plays the scenes or situations of which depend upon animal acting. Several manufacturers maintain menageries! Each studio has a star or two of either sex who is best known for certain types of characters and plays. These high salaried artists must be kept busy. Study their needs!

(c) *Photography*—Such photographic marvels have been accomplished in motography, that the playwright is apt to forget that there is any boundary line to possibility in photographic effects. First of all, there is the matter of color; blue, for instance, becomes white on the screen, and red, black. Black and white alone are resultant except in kinemacolor or in tinted negative. When a situation or dramatic point depends upon color, it will have to be indicated either by caption or by insert. The camera is quicker than the human eye and more unfailing, in that it records everything that passes within its range of focus. Tyros have to be told again and again that exteriors cannot be made at night. The night scene would have to be artificially lighted by a flash, which would result in a daylight effect! Rain, night, lightning, storm and pictures taken in a darkened or over-lighted atmosphere, are

113

usually "effects" artificially created. We do not see, for instance, bona fide lightning descending from the sky and simultaneously striking a man dead. The technical secret of portraying all difficult effects of this kind is by showing them in two or more scenes—*first cause, then effect*. First, we see lightning in the sky; then, we see the man the instant after being struck, collapsing. Night exteriors may be well simulated by having the action isolated under the rays of a street lamp or other direct rays of light, with darkness surrounding. Light and the want of it are the chief obstacles in the way of photography; the genius of the directors and their co-operators have made almost any conceivable "effect" possible. Frequently manuscripts call for exteriors in foreign countries. Very seldom can backgrounds and sets do anything more than make a cheap, wooden presentment of the Eiffel Tower, or the Pyramids or St. Paul's, London. The playwright may accomplish his aim, by keeping his foreign scenes all interiors, with possibly a glimpse of the distant landmark thru the window.

(d) *Manufacturer* — Every manufacturing

company has some producing policy or characteristic. The Kalem, for instance, is noteworthy for its war dramas, Edison for its leaning toward topical themes—and so on. In this relation, it may be well to remember that each company has a staff of salaried playwrights who furnish many of their typical features. The manufacturers both love and hate the spectacular; they feel that it is beloved by the public and the life of competition, yet they abhor the dangers, destructivity and tremendous expense and superhuman effort it entails. Some day they will realize that the public really loves simple drama more than they do sensational spectacle.

3. THE MANUSCRIPT (a) *Technique* —In fiction the deeds need only be probable; in photodrama they must be actually performable, because the audience must see them. For the photoplay must show whatever is vital. Keep your captions down to 15 words at the most, and your inserts to 20, as every word means a foot of film. Tell how your characters shall act, leave to the director where and how they enter and exit. Write mainly about characters that arouse the spectators'

sympathy. Our photoplay is not told, but acted. Photoplay happenings should transpire in the same order as they do in life. There is nothing so unconvincing as a multiplicity of coincidences. First become an expert on words, if you would be a master of thought. Be certain that you state briefly all crises, situations, and the climax in the Synopsis. Be sure that you feel all the emotions you plan to inspire in others and that you have a dramatic idea before you worry about technique.

(b) *Preparation*—Good English is essential to the photoplaywright, not merely because it is the badge of literacy, but because thru good, clear, forceful English alone can the playwright hope to give searching expression to an exquisite impression! Beside being a literary offering, the submission of a manuscript is a purely business venture. We offer our goods for sale; we put them up in an attractively neat parcel; we label them plainly with our name and address in the left-hand corner of the Cast, Synopsis and Scenario sheets only; we prepay the postage of the manuscript both to and from the prospective buyer, sustaining a good impression by inclosing a self-addressed envelope. A carbon copy of a manuscript is the only perfect safeguard in case of loss. The hand-written manuscript is as out-of-date as the hand printing press.

(c) *Sale*—You can not force a firm to buy what it does not want, and it is unbusinesslike to demand reasons or to censure it for its refusal to do so. You will be paid, naturally, what the manuscript is commercially worth and not what it may be valued at by you. You should always be conceded the privilege of refusing an offer, just as the buyer is given the right to buy. A photoplay cannot be copyrighted, thanks to a ludicrous Department of the United States Government. Happily, published works of Literature can—after a fashion—so that the aspiring playwright will do best to photodramatize only such plays, books, short stories and poems as he himself is author of. If you wish to reserve story or stage rights, make it clear in the receipt you sign. The photoplay market has a unique bit of etiquette—for a business transaction—that demands of you to submit your manuscript to but one manufacturer at a time. Sales are influenced, of course, by the excellence of the playwright's product; but they are forced alone by the law of supply and demand.

A few important admonitions remain, chief among which is to eschew the sterile pseudonym of "moving pictures," when photodrama is meant. Furthermore, scorn and cry down the derogatory and ignominious term of "movie" that stands between the playwright and his claim to a dignified profession.

Be original—and you can only acquire the virtue thru a constant attendance at the theaters, seeking what has been worn to triteness and learning what has never been done at all. Observe what "gets the hand," and you will surely find what will get the heart! Be persistent—if you have faith in your play; keep revising it; keep sending it out.

PART II
THE PLOT OF THE PHOTODRAMA

*A photoplay Plot is the unpolished
material for a COMPLETE decisive
action; it is composed of cumulative
and interesting incidents rising to a
dramatic climax, and terminating in
a manner calculated to gratify and
warrant the interest roused in its
beginning.*

CHAPTER I

WHAT PLOT MATERIAL IS*

THE PLOT GERM; THE PREMISE ADVANCED;
ANCIENT THEME AND ORIGINAL TREATMENT.

TO the producer a plot is material capable of being dramatized thru visualized
action into a life-like story. To the play-

---

*"The Plot of the Short Story—an Exhaustive Study,
Both Synthetical and Analytical, with Copious Examples,
Making the Work a Practical Treatise," is recommended to
students desiring to study this important subject exhaust-
ively.

wright a plot is suggestive material capable of being developed into the nucleus of a story.

The average plot builder makes the mistake of looking upon plot material as ready-made plots. He thus confuses plot germ (or material) with complete plot. Plot germs lie about us by the score; complete plots are hidden in the most evasive creases of our imaginative genius. The plot germ is merely an item of suggestive plot material, which may be lost sight of entirely in the search for the logical incidents to complete the plot that is eventually led up to. Plot germs, then, are ready-made; but complete plots are made-to-order.

The source, manifestation and aim of all plots is Man (or humanity), his desires (or passions) and his emotional relationships with his God and his fellow-man. A plot germ is an isolated incident, phase, deed, relationship, fragment, or moment, vitally connected with and suggestive of man's emotional life. A plot germ is seldom used exactly in the form in which it originally presents itself. It is valuable principally as *suggestive* material. Like other germs, it must be pregnant with a life of its own that will vitally affect any other mass upon which its energies are concentrated. Carrying the simile further, we find that plot germs, too, often so change the nature of the ideas they fasten upon, that they lose their own identity in the master idea.

(EXAMPLE 47.) Man's relations with the Devil is in itself plot material, but too general. We must become more particular. Crime is one of man's relationships with the Devil, but that is not available as definite plot material; at least it is not a plot germ as yet. We further particularize, and select sub-divisions of crime: Bomb, Thief and Finger prints. Here again is elemental plot material, but there are further steps still to be taken before we can class them as legitimate plot material, or plot germs. At last, we arrive upon pregnant material— among the items of the daily newspaper—which we can seize upon as plot germs: "Bomb Throwers Trailed by a Boy;" "Caretaker Locked in Closet by a Thief;" and "Take Finger Prints of Everybody."

The discovery of a plot germ, however, merely marks the beginning of the exercise of one's plotting power. This starts our thoughts in a definite train in search of an idea. The idea proves to be something *big* that comes to pass; that is our story. Now we will begin to build our plot by seeking a *cause* for the great deed that culminates the story. That cause becomes the beginning of our play. The effect of the causal condition, ambition or deed, results in the events that happen between the beginning and climax of the play, and raises three standard questions that our complete plot must answer: (1) What is the Cause? (2) What is the Effect of the cause? (3) What Climax does the effect lead to?

A great photoplay plot should concern a ludicrous, a pathetic, an heroic or a tragic episode in the lives of two or more people. A complete plot is, in fact, a perfect syllogism. We advance our first premise for the action to follow in the Cause; our second premise is the Effect, or action; there can be but one conclusion, which we demonstrate in the Climax.

Original themes are few in number and were all used scores and scores of times before this generation was born; original plots are inexhaustible and admit of as many variations as there are products in literature from different minds based upon the original twenty-six letters of the alphabet. Do not be afraid of the ancient theme, because the fact that it still survives shows its popular sway; but your survival as a playwright depends on your originality in treatment of plot material in its application to theme.

*Plot material is the tell-tale dust of
Deeds that lies heavy behind the curtain of Commonplace Events; in the
crevices pried open by Ambition; in
the niches worn by Crime; and in
the knot-holes gnarled by Nature.*

CHAPTER II

WHERE TO GET PLOT GERMS

OBSERVATION; READING; EMPLOYMENT OF
FACTS; THE DAILY NEWSPAPER; DANGERS;
PROPRIETY; ORIGINALITY; THE "TRUE
STORY;" IMPORTANCE OF NOTES; TITLES;
PLOT CLASSIFICATION.

DAILY life is filled with dull routine and
monotonous detail; but drama is contrary to actual life, in that it picks and chooses
the events it requires for its purposes, isolat-
ing, magnifying and suppressing them according to its needs. Drama demands that
there be a keynote of human interest, a bond
of vital relationship, in the life of man, or the
revealment of a soul's supreme moment under pressure of struggle.

To have one's eyes open in his search for plot material is not sufficient; the plot seeker's imagination must be sensitively alert, and his emotions prepared to throw some feeling into the impression. Thus equipped, he may acquire *visions* thru observation, and not mere mental photographs. Bear in mind that this matter of creating Literature and Drama draws just as heavily on the emotions as it does on brains. The imagination is the frontier post between the two.

(EXAMPLE 48.) A plot germ resulting from observation: A man sits in his office looking out of the window when a blinding flash assails his eyes. It proves to be a boy passing the window opposite with a bright can in his hand which refracted the sun. A plot germ instantly suggests itself: He visions an old house, set back from the road; surrounded by shrubbery; he is the hero who sits in his own home some distance away; the flash; he gets his glasses and sees a woman in distress—there is productive material for a play. Scarcely a vestige of the original suggestive matter remains.

It is more beneficial for a student of literature or drama to associate with the works of a master than with the master himself. Few successful artists are successful teachers; their success lies in their having absorbed and *forgotten* technique. Thus in hearing and seeing drama and reading literature, the promising student should normally feel all that is noble and great within him rise—like a host on the wings of inspiration—to meet and do honor to the master creatures of thought and feeling created by the playwright and author. Exaltation is the coveted gateway to inspiration, thru which every artist-creator must pass.

(EXAMPLE 49.) A visit to the drama might yield a plot germ in the following manner: Let us say we saw Douglas Fairbank's noteworthy impersonation of Bertie in "The New Henrietta." We were inspired at once with a story surrounding "The Boy Who Couldn't Be Bad"—which is the title and theme of our incipient play.

In employing facts to any large degree, the photoplaywright will encounter danger in two particulars: (1) The more *commonplace* the plot material, the more subtile the dramatic art necessary to make it attractive as a play; (2) The more *extraordinary* the fact material, the greater the tact requisite to make it seem plausibly real. The simple rule is, Dramatize

your facts before you employ them! Develop
the dramatic habit in all your five senses; better still, create a sixth and call it the Sense
of Drama.

Little tragedies, romances and dramas are
constantly happening in the circles of people
with whom we come in daily contact—therein
lies danger, however. More than a mere
change of scene or character is necessary.
The actual, intimate happening must form, if
employed in any degree, but a suggestive plot
germ, or only an episode in an entirely *new
story*. The best way to avoid disaster in this
relation is to see to it that the development
and elaboration of your resultant plot is not
the same as that of the incident upon which
it was based.

*(EXAMPLE 50.) The almost daily sight of an
old character who is brow-beaten by his entire family,
inspires speculation as to how he lost his nerve and
prestige, possibly a fortune too? For the purpose
of our plot, we say that he gambled away his fortune. He had a theory of beating the market. He
and his wealthy son-in-law become friends, and before anyone realizes it he has induced his son-in-law
to put his whole fortune back of the old theory!*

The daily newspaper is perhaps the most

prolific source of plot germs. Take special note that this does not mean *complete* plots. The question of originality arises—for suppose other seekers choose the same news clipping for development? In answer to this, it may be said that not two persons in a thousand—providing they employ only the suggestive germ and do not try to follow verbatim the news story—will take the same point of view, will assume the same mood, will employ the same plot development, or will choose the same plot manifestation. True originality consists in doing the much-done thing in a new way. Be sure that you are not trite, then go ahead.

The newspaper is most useful, perhaps, as a source of novel situations, which are in constant demand in the development of the photoplay. We arrive at a pass in the progressive building of our plot and find that we are about to use an incident that has been worn threadbare. If our press clippings are classified, all we have to do is to turn to the proper classification, and in all probability we will make a discovery worth while.

(*EXAMPLE 51.*) *Suppose we are seeking some*

new way of catching a thief, some of the following ought to be illuminating: (1) Clue to Leegson Murder; (2) Join Dictograph to Telephone; (3) Police Hoax Brings Gunmen's Capture; (4) Women Sleuths Catch a Fugitive; (5) Bomb Throwers Trailed by a Boy. Here are five items of plot material, plot germs and dramatic situations.

Beware of "true stories" as plots. They lack the essential ingredients of the fiction story, or dramatized play. They are loaded with deadly personal detail that is usually too localized for the world-sweep of the photodrama. They need most of their prime facts ripped out and to be larded with choice bits of invented detail. True stories make excellent anecdotes; but not one in a thousand bears any resemblance to a complete photoplay plot.

Plot material is useless unless it is stored in sufficient quantities to enable the consulting plot seeker to make use of it without being cramped in his selection. Photoplaywriting is too arduous labor to resort to slip-shod methods such as trying to remember items of plot material. It is part of the author's business to store up energy and ideas. The application of a simple system, along the line of that which follows, will permit the playwright to catalog, classify and file all of his plot material (notes, clippings, pictures, etc.) in a manner that will enable him to file or find any conceivable item instantaneously.

(EXAMPLE 52.) This classified plot directory and catalog is elastic and universal. The ambitious student may readily carry it to completion along the lines indicated. There are easily a thousand subdivisions possible. There are 7 grand divisions: (I) The Heart of Man; (II) The Ambition of Man; (III) The Flesh of Man; (IV) The Soul of Man; (V) The Mind of Man; (VI)Not-Man; (VII) Humor. We will divide but one of these grand divisions: (I) THE HEART OF MAN—(1) Man; (2) Woman; (3) Love; (4) Marriage; (5) Children; (6) Family; (7) Home; (8) Friendship; (9) Separation; (10) Reunion. The sub-divisions of (4) Marriage: (a) Name; (b) Money; (c) Bigamy; (d) Deception; (e) Beauty; (f) Blunder; (g) Runaway; (h) Micegination; (i) Morganatic; (j) Eugenics.

A final suggestion as a source of plot material (as well as a harvesting of titles for plays and stories) is a persistent search for, and a diligent setting down for future use, of happy phrases, which may be heard, read or conceived by the playwright. He will find that a large percentage of these phrase-titles are the nucleus of plots in themselves. In most cases they suggest the coveted big story.

(EXAMPLE 53.) *The Tides of Fate; When a Man Cannot Pay; Give Him a Chance; Somebody Had to Do It; To Those That Have; Who Live in the Past; The Quality of Youth; For A' That; For Good and All; One Chance in a Hundred.*

Plot material is the stuff that souls are made of; it is the composition from which careers are moulded; it is sparks from the forge of nobility and salt distilled from the tears of humanity. Plot material means a record of man's activities outside of the four dull walls of Convention and beyond the dominion of the Commonplace.

The great principle that governs the construction, outcome and solution of all organizations, plans and plots, is the ever-conscious FORE-KNOWLEDGE AND FORE-SHADOWING of the objective mission, the sum of all the parts and the decisive action

CHAPTER III

BEGINNING WITH THE END

SEEKING THE CLIMAX; WHEN TO BEGIN THE PHOTOPLAY; EVER-FORWARD MOVEMENT; THE LIVE BEGINNING.

THE great question in the minds of the audience is, What will be the outsome of it all? Audiences generally take all beginnings of plays for granted. No ambitious playwright, however, can afford to take and employ plot beginnings as a mere matter of chance. Every particle employed in the building of a plot is the part of a conscious, pre-arranged design—most especially the beginning.

132

In the first place, we must find something to write about; some condition, experience or deed that is worthy of a plot, a story or a play. As we consider this or that item of plot material, in our search for a plot germ, we pause and ask of it: To what end? To what good? The moment we discern the culmination of a big moment, or the performance of a decisive action, or the accomplishment of a great deed, we have found our plot germ. This is not the beginning of our play, but its culmination, or climax. We at once set about to clarify, strengthen and heighten this climax. The process should fill us with inspiration, give our thoughts the impetus of flight and point our course clear and straight. Thus inspired, equipped and confident, we set out to begin our play.

(EXAMPLE 54.) We may peruse newspapers, read books, witness plays and give our attention to plot material in vain and then stumble over a pregnant plot germ in an unexpected quarter. For instance, we suddenly discern in our old neighbor whom we have seen around all our life, a picture of tragedy, that echoes Lear. He had slouched around the place, scolded by his wife and brow-beaten by the grown children until he seemed the acme of the common-

*place. Tears in his eyes one day suggest a story.
He was the plot material; his tears the plot germ;
how to make the old man happy in the last great moment of his life, is the climax and aim of the prospective play.*

The climax resolves itself into a definite
purpose to guide the playwright; for he writes
every scene with a view to its influence on the
climax; if it has no influence on the climax,
that is sufficient evidence that it is not necessary for his play purposes. The writer who
sits down to write his play with no definite
idea of the outcome is bound to be swayed
by every new development that appears on the
horizon of his imagination. His characters
will lead him around by the ears, tweak his
nose and play blind man's bluff with him—
as the resultant play will show.

We begin our photoplay with the incident
that marks the beginning of the vital relationship between one of the principal characters and the climax. The birth of the plot,
however, does not mean the birth of the characters. The ever-forward trend necessitates
our going back only once—when we begin.

(EXAMPLE 55.) To resume our plot of Example

54: Having resolved on the climax to bring the affairs of our old-man hero to the greatest moment of his life, we must turn now from the facts entirely and weave our fiction tale: The old man in his youth was a gambler; he lost the fortune for which his wife married him; he won his family's everlasting disregard; he had always had a "system" which he knew could beat the market; this is what they all say; one of his daughters marries a well-to-do, genial young man; he becomes the old man's friend; the old man confides his "system" to him and manages to make him believe in it; these two plan to invest all he has; they do; the family discover it too late; they drive him out; the son-in-law's fortune is apparently lost; the tide turns and he wins a fabulous amount; it is he who brings the old man back—ready to die now that he has proved his precious "system." Since our play concerns the old man's relations with his son-in-law, we may properly begin it just previous to that young man's engagement with his daughter. Our first scene could be captioned: "Ill-treated Half His Life for Losing the Money Ma Married Him For." The action would establish the old man's relations with his family. To go back to the old man's losing his fortune would be to run the risk of telling another story and necessitates the "years later" breach in the development.

By a live beginning we mean one that quickly gets into the heart of the theme with as few scenes as possible. It can be done in the first scene very often, especially if preceded by a meaty caption. The first scene must be suggestive at least of the climax.

(EXAMPLE 56.) In the first scene of "All Power for a Day" we establish the irrascible character of Col. Farrington that led to his attack on Ridgway and his death that brought about the big moment of the play . . . In "The Salt of Vengeance" the first scene depicts Dalton discovering the rotten bridge that later precipitated the train that maimed his child and caused him to seek vengeance. . . . In "The Master of the Lost Hills" the letter is screened that jilts Shelburne and sends him out to the Lost Hills on the great adventure that makes the play.

Our course lies between beginning the play too early and injuring the continuity by "years-later" breaks; or not beginning it soon enough and having to resort to explanations, thru hitching visions, of many important scenes depending upon something that has gone before. Try to begin at that point where the first scene in the vital action occurs; make the identities powerful and clear; establish relationships that nothing will efface from the minds of the audience. Then go ahead with as little loss of time as possible, for the audience is apt to be skeptical at first and sit back demanding, "Well?"

Every scene should develop the plot a step in advance and contribute to the climax, or it has no reason for being in the play.

CHAPTER IV

Development and Continuity

EACH SCENE CONTRIBUTES TO CLIMAX; ELE-
MENT OF TIME AND CHRONOLOGICAL SE-
QUENCE; PROBLEMS OF CONTINUITY; THE
CENTRAL THEME; THE RETURN; INSTAN-
TANEOUS SEQUENCE; TIME INDICATIVES.

A S we have learned, that which happens in our play happens NOW. All time is present time, therefore all things must happen chronologically correct. Whatever period of time we carry our audience back to in our first scene constitutes the beginning of all things, as far as our present purpose is concerned. Affairs relentlessly and inevitably move forward. In this relation, special care must be taken in the screening of simultaneous action in different scenes. Perfect continuity can be maintained always by having the contributory scenes obviously bear upon the principal theme, or that which is held in suspense.

(EXAMPLE 57.) In "The Master of the Lost Hills" our principal scenes are those picturing the hero himself. The contributing scenes are those showing the peril that threatens him. Scene 95 discloses Shelburne dodging missiles as he barricades door; 96 shows angry mob outside; 97 gives a rear view of the house showing his personal enemy building a fire against shack. Subsequent deeds follow this simultaneous action.

In the photoplay we have no wait, as in stage drama, while the scenes are being shifted, therefore we must have perfect continuity of time. We cannot digress with irrelevant matter; we must fill in with contributive material always. An episode is an isolated incident that has no place in the photoplay. The plot begins with the cause of it all and can never pause until it has arrived at a satisfactory solution. Lapses of time should never appear to be gaps or voids, but become well rounded periods suggestively filled by artistic construction. We have seen how only forward or simultaneous action can win conviction of actuality. A very fine phase

139

of this principle is essential when a vital causal action demands an immediate view of the effect. In other words, instantaneous sequences must follow instantaneously.

(EXAMPLE 58.) A man is about to commit suicide in one scene; he lifts the revolver—the next scene shows his frivolous wife, the cause of it all; laughing and chatting in the next room; she springs up suddenly in horror—another scene shows the instant following the shooting. Or, a man breaking thru a door in one scene, appears instantly in the next scene.

This method of showing immediate continuity is also employed to accelerate action and maintain suspense. It is called the "cutback," which term has the objectionable quality of suggesting "going back." What we do is to revisit, or *return,* to a scene previously screened. The strict application of the "cutback"—or Return, as we shall hereafter designate it—is in the case of a rapid sequence of action wherein the Return reoccurs for an extended period in almost every other scene. We find its abuse in the "chase" picture, which by some directors is still considered drama. Rarely we find that one scene need sustain the action for a longer period than is apt to be interestingly safe. In that case we must break up the scene with one or more Returns of another scene, or action, that has a contributive effect on the thematic scene which we have broken. A long scene may be broken effectively by the insertion of a Close-view. All of these constructive possibilities must be resorted to in building the effective plot. In other words, we must test each scene by visualizing it before we write it out. Our rough draft is our plot, that may be changed to meet, create and strengthen dramatic exigencies. Remember that we must suggest even more than fiction, since we must tell the director and actor what must be done, as well as show the audience a moving drama!

Definite actions, or tasks, that take considerable time in the execution, are readily encompassed by the Return, or the introduction of new material of a cumulative nature.

(EXAMPLE 59.) A mob's march of a mile or so; the burning of a house containing prisoners; the digging of a tunnel in order to escape; the cutting down of a tree in which the hero is perched—progressive stages in the task are shown, alternating with scenes bearing upon the result that readily present themselves to the playwright.

A play should progress even when it appears to go back. This seeming paradox is concerned especially with the employment of the Vision. It means that every scene should contribute action—and every insert supply data—that advance the play *in the mind of the audience,* by indirectly clearing away some obstacle that has stood in the way of its further progress, or by supplying material that heightens lingering suspense, or by directly adding new action that impetuously drives the development toward a climax.

(EXAMPLE 60.) In "The Lost Melody" we are shown, thru a vision, the picture that is passing thru Douglas's mind NOW; its presence was necessary to clear away the great obstacle that barred Douglas's reformation (the Climax); the play bounded forward in interest as it was visualized.

We do not advance far in the construction of our photoplay plot before we realize that variety is the spice of its life. Simplicity of theme is essential, but simplicity of plot seems out of the question. This, in a large measure, is true. It is the parting of the ways from the short story, for in that the single, simple plot is essential; in the photoplay the complicated

142

plot is not only best but next to essential in creating cumulative suspense. Our theme should be so simple that we may state it in a few words. It is the subject-matter of the play; the Climax is its direct outcome; our hero is with it thru thick and thin because his body and soul are made of it; it is the play. *All else is contributive matter.* The theme is comparable to the main line of a railroad that is fed and sustained by way-stations and branch lines; if we expect to reach an important destination we can arrive only by way of the main line.

Continuing this view of the complications as tributary material suggests a method of plot building that has exceptional merits. We shall call it the building by dramatic sequences.

(EXAMPLE 61.) We shall quote "The Coming of the Real Prince," in this connection again. A sequence includes a definite section of action marking the dramatic crises in the play. In the instance of this play a caption has designated each sequence. 1. Annie's Widowed Mother Left Penniless Opens a Boarding House; 2. Better Times But No Sympathy From a Busy Mother; 3. Annie Finds Solace in "Cinderella"; etc. We take 1. Annie's Widowed

Mother Left Penniless and append all the tributary scenes we can conceive; possibly not in the exact order in which they are finally employed; (a) Arrival home after the funeral; (b) Failure of the boarding house; (c) Servants discharged; (d) Annie becomes the drudge. And so on, in each sequence until the Climax is reached.

The only rule is to keep as close to the central theme as possible, for the completed action must be so perfectly woven that all matter fits as a perfect whole with no suggestion of patches, so artistically is the construction hidden.

The element of time is the secret of logical sequence in the photoplay—always make certain that the following scene is without question the scene that follows. Perfect continuity insures perfect illusion.

One of the big little problems that lies before the playwright is to invent a time indicative without the monotonous mention of time at all—at least by means of such trite Captions as "The Next Day," "Two Years Later," "That Night," etc. Lapses of time in the continuity of essential action are inevitable. It is vitally necessary to an appreciation of the dramatic significance of a scene that the

144

audience know whether a day or a year has elapsed. The Caption alone proves to be the only reliable source of information. The real difficulty lies in eliminating the aforementioned type of time indicative.

(EXAMPLE 62.) The solution seems to rest in incorporating time significance to the entire Caption phrase, or at least in transposing the actual time words from an isolated position to a relative place in the Caption itself. Instead of, "The Next Day. Ridgway Returns Tho Forbidden Ever to Trespass;" why not, "Tho Forbidden Ever to Trespass Ridgway Returns the Next Day"? It is infinitely stronger. "Alice Reconciled to Fate HAS BECOME Gov. Marsten's Secretary." "Mrs. Dalton Learns the Truth AFTER TWO MONTHS' Deception." "AFTER the Operation." "SUMMER Brings Hope for Dalton." (The capitalization is for the student's benefit only.)

Plot building is simply carrying a dramatic premise to a dramatic conclusion.

*In the Beginning of the Plot we
have seen the Cause; in its Development we have felt the Effect of that
cause; in the Climax we cannot avoid
its inevitable Consequence.*

CHAPTER V

The Climax and Completed Plot

SEQUENCE AND CONSEQUENCE; LOGICAL CAUSE
AND COMPLETE SOLUTION; SUSTAINED CLI-
MAX; ALL EXPECTATIONS FULFILLED.

W E have learned that we must create interest with the very first scene by significant action, and that our characters must
win admiration or dislike upon their first appearance, but the fond hopes that we create in
the beginning and excite thruout the development of the play must not be gratified till the
Climax is reached. Nevertheless, thru pains-
taking construction, it is usually the unexpected that happens in the Climax, tho always
that which is logical and has been the secret
desire of the audience. A premise once ad-

146

vanced in the beginning of the plot must be conclusively proved, right or wrong, in the issue of the Climax; that is all there is to the play.

(EXAMPLE 63.) In the plot introduced in Example 53, we picture the old man in such a way that he wins the audience's immediate sympathy and thus premise and promise to do all in our play-power to win his emancipation from abuse. We make the audience hope that he will win out with his "system" that once lost his fortune. To put every obstacle we can in his path marks the dramatic development of the plot; to remove them is the part of the Climax —providing it is not designed to be a tragedy.

Climax brings the suspense to its summit and determines the outcome of the play in a single scene. What follows should be rapidly disposed of, and constitutes the Conclusion. The most effective drama is that which concludes with and is one with the Climax. This leaves an impression with the audience that minor details in a drawn-out Conclusion often efface.

(EXAMPLE 64.) In "The Salt of Vengeance," the Climax comes in Scene 39; Dalton makes a superhuman effort to wave his handkerchief with the speeding train bearing down on him. 40 shows the

*cab of the engine, closing the throttle just in time.
41 shows the Climax still sustained but waning;
Dalton has collapsed and the little girl whom he had
risked his life to save, running toward him. 42 is the
real Conclusion taken some time later with inimical
factions all united in perfect happiness. In "All
Power for a Day," we find the Climax and Conclusion synomynous; Marsten, who has hampered, jailed
and almost had our hero executed for a murder he
himself had committed. The release of the hero and
accusation drives him to suicide. The hero claims
the heroine and they are handed a telegram for
Marsten which tells them that Marsten has won that
for which he had labored all his life—he is dead; it
is the hero who holds all things. That is the end of
the play.*

That our characters are married, have children and live happily forever after, are separate outgrowths of our present play and require a new plot to handle any story they may
contain. The play deals solely with removing
the obstacles that stand in the way of our
hero in his accomplishment of a definite object. The obstacles once removed, his object
must be within his grasp, if the play is properly plotted. Preliminary to the Climax, the
plot deck must be cleared for a decisive action; minor characters must be disposed of

and nothing permitted to interfere with the titanic struggle for supremacy between the hero and his foes. The instant one or other receives the mortal blow, our plot has achieved its purpose; our tale is told; our play is over.

PART IIII
DRAMATIC CONSTRUCTION OF THE PHOTOPLAY

Drama is the presentation of man laboring under the stress of an Emotion that personifies Pathos; a Passion that flames into Struggle; or a Desire that embodies itself in Deeds —sufficiently entertaining and edifying to make mankind pause, feel, think and be benefited.

CHAPER I

DRAMA AND PHOTODRAMA

DEFINITION ; PRINCIPLES ; STRUCTURE IS EVERY-THING; THE DRAMATIC IDEA; EMOTION IS THE SECRET; DESIRE THE MOTIVE POWER; DRAMA AND MELODRAMA.

PHOTODRAMA is—as we all know—a coherent series of animated photographs projected life-like and life-size on a screen, realistically visualizing a dramatic story. The one word "animated" eliminates forever the authority to employ the word "picture" in this relation. "Moving pictures" or "motion pictures" may be pictures that are standing, or moving, or dancing, or jumping—for all the adjective suggests—but it is impossible to make the term synonymous with photodrama. It is, to say the least, a misnomer that misleads —especially the playwright. Photodrama is not pictures, but *life!*

The man who writes photoplays should study and master the principles of dramatic construction. Before all things he is a playwright. Later he will learn that photodrama is the older dramatic art and something beside, requiring a new type and a new school of artists. He will learn that what is in demand with fiction and stage drama is in vogue with the photodrama. He should realize by this time that dramatic art is both a faithful reflection of the vital and contemporaneous emotional, mental and spiritual life of the civilized world, and an appeal to the elemental passions of humanity. With the perpetuating of existing literature and drama in photoplay form, the independent playwright will have little to do, as this work usually falls to the lot of the staff writer. It is collaborative rather than creative work.

As plot is the science of structure, so dramatics is the art of treatment. Plot is a matter of selection; drama one of application of the selected material. We take it for granted that all plot material is inherently—tho crudely, perhaps—dramatic. We hint at both plot and treatment when we state that drama is a supreme human experience interpreted by characters in terms of emotion with piercing effect. It is the clash of soul against soul in visualized struggle. It is spiritual conflict. It is not the contention of ideas merely, for that could be expressed only in words; nor is it the strife of matter, for that could be expressed only in dynamic and spectacular action—it is a clash of interests that involves both.

(EXAMPLE 65.) In the play "The Struggle" (Kalem) the methods of producers in going out of their way to make spectacle of drama is shown. The plot was built on the idea of the struggle of Labor against Capital, which in itself is essentially dramatic. The dramatic construction developed two characters symbolizing their respective classes. The contrast was essentially dramatic. They were made to see—

not each other's strength to crush and kill, but each other's power of human kindness under the test of sympathy. That was the idea of the author. The following line on the posters shows that the producers had ideas of their own which substituted spectacle for drama: "See the great iron mill in operation and the sensational rescue from fire!" Neither of these contingencies had been a part of the original play!

Thus we find our first essential is to make sure that our plot germ is dramatic. Our plot development has conditions and needs of its own that carry us forward logically to the point of successful treatment. Finally, we are prepared to proceed with our dramatic construction, which is to convert a mechanical framework into an appealing play. Plot construction is a matter of form; dramatic construction one of effect. Provided the plot construction is excellent, dramatic construction resolves itself into the task of arrangement and re-arrangement of the matter contained in the plot.

The secret of all dramatic effects is emotional impression on the audience. To endure, such an impression must contain a big dramatic idea; one that involves an emotional experience that, *under the given circumstances,* might happen to anybody anywhere. Love, Sacrifice, Honor, Reconciliation, Re-union and Retribution are a few of the great themes that never fail to stir the hearts of audiences the world over. The success of the photoplay-wright lies in his dramatic skill and originality in weaving new situations from old relationships.

Addison's statement of the nature and quali-fications of drama still stands: "First, there must be one action; secondly, it must be an entire action; thirdly, it must be a great action."

Melodrama is pure drama exaggerated. The hero and the heroine are very, very good; the villain and the adventuress are very, very bad; their manner is extraordinarily vio-lent; their method is to startle both the audi-ence and each other by their actions and deeds; all emotion with them is passion; they accomplish superhuman tasks and are gener-ally untrue to all conception of real life. Daring spectacle is one of their favorite re-sources.

Actions are only the Alphabet of Drama, which must be spelt into critical Words of Emotion and coherent Sentences of Suspense before they express Deeds—the common Language and Bond of all human heart Interest.

CHAPTER II

DRAMATIC EXPRESSION

THE LAWS OF MOVEMENT AND ACTION; CHARACTER AND MOTIVE; RELATION TO AUDIENCE AND CHARACTER; DRAMATIC VERSUS DYNAMIC; REALISM, ROMANTICISM AND IDEALISM.

IN drama we make no attempt to reproduce facts, but to induce reality. Illusion is all things. The dramatist deliberately sets about to make the hour that an audience gives to seeing his play become one of the greatest events in their emotional history. He does not merely imitate or mimic life, he *lives* the life, and then, thru his dramatic and technical skill—or Art—translates it into such familiar terms that all who see can understand.

155

Strictly speaking, action is but the external conduct of the characters, or actors. Great danger lies in the playwright's failure to understand and appreciate the marked difference between movement and action. Movement is the internal undercurrent of real dramatic progression. That actors come and go rapidly across the screen, or that their actions shall be violent or punctuated with gestures, is not by any means sufficient. Actions must express and portray an internal struggle with which the audience is in sympathetic understanding. There must be an underlying emotional meaning for every prominent action that is displayed on the screen. Thus the dramatic element is perceived by the audience thru its effect upon the characters and their consequent actions. This is called motive, as well as movement; it begins and continues in the guise of cumulative insinuations from the very first scene, reaching its full stage of development in the climax. This requires the most skillful and technical execution on the part of the playwright, who must throw his whole soul into it without once showing his hand. In other words, dramatic effects must come about as naturally as the normal actions of the characters. Too often photoplays are nothing more than a series of continued pictures, any-one or more of which might be cut out with-out affecting the final scene. To the contrary, drama is a living thing, and amputation will either maim, or mar, or kill it outright.

(EXAMPLE 66.) A single scene from a play in which a girl who has discovered and developed a talent in a man is thrown off by him in the moment of his triumph, shows the difference between Move-ment and Action: (Action) Forbes is standing in the center of the room, the lion of the hour; ladies crowding around him in excited contest; one seems to get the major share of attention. (Movement) Alica, the heroine, enters with joy and pride on her face; steps forward to shake his hand; at first he pretends he does not know her; then accompanies his handshake with a curt nod; turning away almost rudely to the other woman. . . . Showing that the chief difference lies in action affecting the character and movement affecting the audience.

Movement, then, is that which is felt more than it is seen. It brings us face to face again with the power of suggestion, which is one of the secret springs of dramatic effects. By means of it everything is made to play a dramatic part in our drama.

(EXAMPLE 67.) In a scene picturing the hour a man has selected to declare his love, we find a moonlight effect; they sing a love song; "the time, the place and the girl" are all harmonious. . . . In another scene we depict this man's poverty by showing his threadbare room; there are many suggestions of better days; his manner shows refinements that suggest his former affluence and make his surroundings pathetically dramatic.

The finer points in dramatic construction are equivalent—and just as necessary—as those of fiction narration. Dramatic construction and expression are modulated according to the nature of the theme. Realism, Romanticism and Idealism each has its methods of producing effects. We must guard against the vulgarity of ultra-realism and bear in mind that all idealism must be edifying and romanticism refined. Realism is materialistic and calls for gross details and convincing spectacle; Romanticism is luxuriant and revels in the vagaries of youth, the desire for love and the intoxication of adventure; Idealism is delicate and speculates in beauty, dreams and perfection. The three are like solids, oil and water that can never mix. If our play be a romance, its contributive elements must be

158

romantic to produce the desired romantic effect.

(EXAMPLE 68.) The three plays following are examples of Realism, Romanticism and Idealism, as their titles appropriately suggest: "The Salt of Vengeance," "The Coming of the Real Prince" and "The Lost Melody." The first is a play of revenge and does not mince matters in delineating it; there is a wreck, a thrilling hold-up scene and a sacrifice involving bloodshed. The second shows the blowing and bursting of the romantic bubble of a visionary country girl. The third depicts the effect of a youthful ideal upon a man later in life.

There are grave dangers, as we have hinted, in substituting dynamic or spectacular action for dramatic movement, as illustrated in the foregoing chapter by Example 65. Even melodrama can be ruined by it. The toppling over of a house, the realistic battle between two armies, or the smashing of two locomotives, obliterates the fine mechanism of the drama with a realism that satiates and makes everything that follows insipid. The play, the characters and the audience are lost in the debris both literally and artistically. Our object in dramatic expression is to enthrall, not to paralyze. Every distraction of attention

159

from the elemental mediums of pure art is an obstacle thrown into the clear channel of receptivity. Spectacles are for the most part acts that concern themselves and not *deeds* that are an intrinsic part of the drama. The characters and the action step back as it were, while the precipitated spectacle usurps the stage and the attention. Unlike the circus, drama has no legitimate side-shows. We are not interested in anything that happens or that a character may do, but only in what his action indicates and reveals of the story. Spectacles are real "moving pictures"; what we want is moving drama. True drama appeals to the heart; spectacular theatrics assault the nerves.

We should employ the spectacle then, not as an adjunct to drama, but as a vital necessity—which will be rarely. When you can honestly say that what you have written is good drama, and that you cannot do without one or more spectacular scenes, then make use of them by all means.

Suspense marks each dramatic Situation, and consists in retarding its Crisis and withholding its solution as long as it is feasible.

CHAPTER III

SEQUENCE AND SUSPENSE

CAUSE AND EFFECT; EFFECTS DUE TO ARRANGE-
MENT; THE RAW COINCIDENCE; SUSPENSE
MOTORS; BATTLE OF OPPOSING MOTIVES; MO-
TIVE AS WELL AS IDEA.

SEQUENCE in photodrama may almost without exception be called consequence, so continuous and binding are the presence and relationship of cause and effect thruout the photoplay. The very first scene must contain a definite cause, followed by more or less suspense until the effect is revealed. Each effect develops a new cause for suspense which accumulates in volume—if skillfully constructed —until it becomes an almost unendurable burden of expectation, speculation and anxiety in the Climax, or biggest Situation, wherein it is effectively solved.

(EXAMPLE 69.) In the first scene of "The Master of the Lost Hills," the hero's fiancée writes him that she is jilting him. This is really the cause of the entire play that does not find complete solution until the last scene. The second scene of the play shows us the effect of the first upon the hero. Hard hit, he turns from his irresponsible life. Seeing his valet sending annual gifts to the poor whites on his Southern estate becomes the cause of which his sudden departure to the estate of Lost Hills in person is the effect. The startling adventures that follow are the logical consequences.

Unless scenes are fragmentary, that is mere supplementary "flashes," an analysis will disclose a uniformity of development, that has a counterpart in the structure of the play itself, namely: Introduction, Situation, Crisis and Solution.

(EXAMPLE 70.) We take a scene from "All Power for a Day," wherein Ridgway is discovered by his sweetheart with a gun in his hand and suspected of killing her father who lies dying on the floor: (Introduction) Servants rushing in; Ridgway discovered with smoking revolver in his hand gazing dully at Colonel who lies writhing on floor. . . . (Situation) Alice enters, rushes to father's side. He points accusingly at Ridgway. . . . (Suspense) Ridgway comes forward pleadingly; Alice hesitates and starts at what her father is saying; at length nods

162

yes. . . . (Crisis) Alice repulses Ridgway with a gesture; father falls back dead. . . . (Solution—at least of the scene in hand) The sheriff enters and arrests Ridgway.

The progressive effects of scene or play are due to arrangement, as may readily be seen. Each minor effect, tho begun in the first scene, must heighten and tighten the Climax. It accomplishes this by bearing constantly and cumulatively upon the main theme of the play. No matter how many contributive scenes may be necessary, the main theme, or medium, must again predominate. We should engender suspense by so arranging incidents that a vital desire is manifested in the character first; many things may happen before the next unit of sustaining suspense rises—Opportunity to gratify the Desire; the third unit of prolonging suspense is the Frustration of the Opportunity to gratify the Desire. On the other hand, suspense is terminated immediately by the advent of Change, Decision or Fulfillment. The instant that the playwright feels that suspense is being overstrained, he should bring it to a close. The minor incidents of suspense are not closed, however, until they have disposed of themselves by contributing an element of suspense to the main theme that will be felt in the climax itself. For, after all, suspense is merely a suspension of the Climax; each suspension is marked by a crisis, or minor climax. We sustain interest by suspending the Climax.

In drama nothing should be left to motiveless chance, or raw coincidence. Suspense is a promissory note to the audience that the culmination they have been waiting for is worth while, and not a hoax by the author or a termination by an "act of God."

(EXAMPLE 71.) Writers often get their characters in a dilemma that defies solution on their part, upon which an unsuspected treasure is made to appear; or an unhinted-at rescuing party helps the author and hero out; or someone "marries the girl" rather than leave her unprovided for at the conclusion of the play; or it becomes necessary to kill off the unpunished villain or hero-who-has-gone-to-the-bad.

Suspense is much stronger than mere expectation. We may say that expectation is the hope that something will happen; *suspense is the fear that something may happen.* Suspense is not always occasioned by the emotional strain of the character; that is only tension of action. If there is an emotional strain on the audience, then there is sheer suspense. The most dramatic suspense is possible thru the suggestion of impending catastrophe of which the character is blithely and emotionally ignorant, but of which the audience has seen ominous portents in alternating scenes. Thus, in photoplay, we are permitted the excitement of seeing the progress of both sides in the battle of opposing motives. For in drama we must have the swiftly-moving motive as well as the big idea. The course of dramatic sequence follows the line of this motive, the only deviations being those made for the purpose of creating suspense.

Contrast is the essence of all striking Situations—meaning a contrast between characters or their conditions or environments, resulting from or leading to relations between them.

CHAPTER IV

THE POTENTIAL SITUATION

CONTRAST; SITUATION'S RELATION TO AUDIENCE; HARVESTING SITUATIONS; PERIL AND DEATH; CLIMAX AND PUNCH.

THE most poignant dramatic effect is that obtained by contrasting a character with his most coveted—tho ungratified—condition. The most powerful situations are those in which a character is confronted with that which should have been, that which might might have been, or that which can never be. Therein we plunge into the deepest wells of pathos.

(EXAMPLE 72.) As a case of that which should have been, we find the man who failed suddenly coming into the presence of the man who is prosper-

ous because of his failures. That which might have been, we see illustrated in the man and woman meeting years later—the husband and wife of others— when a silly misunderstanding is all that separated them. That which can never be is pathetically shown by an old man making the acquaintance of a youth, who alone can accomplish what he himself wishes to do. These are all dramatic situations of the highest order.

Since drama is an artistic process of obtaining striking and gratifying effects upon the emotions of an audience, the situation is the most frequent and positive means to that end. The situation is what lends novelty, fire and brilliancy to the progressive units of the play. It places the characters in a galvanic relationship with each other or with their condition or environment. It means the introduction of the unexpected—either from the point of view of the character or of the audience. Its introduction marks the beginning of Suspense, and raises the question, What will he do about it? For it means a relationship about which something must be done immediately, and that something is a Crisis. The Situation itself is of short duration but of tremendous power and effect. It succeeds the introductory action, or a sudden revealment to the audience, of which the character may remain in ignorance, or an unlooked-for entry, or an undreamed-of relationship disclosed—that suddenly change the whole aspect of development.

(EXAMPLE 73.) A woman's old father has sent for the police to arrest the young criminal whom he has raised from a foundling—when the daughter discloses that the boy is her illegitimate son, and his grandson! A girl betrays a man to the mob for murdering her wealthy benefactor whom she has never seen—when it is seemingly too late the man proves to her that he is the benefactor, and that her brother murdered his valet! In both cases the audience was aware of the relationship and reveled in the characters' embarrassment.

The foregoing Example has touched a point that should be driven home. It concerns the extent to which the author shall take the audience into his confidence. In this relation, writers will have to discard in photoplay writing what in story writing is undoubtedly one of their greatest assets; namely, the withholding of some of the important details in order to build the delightful surprise at the end. In the photoplay we must take the audience into our confidence, for the simple reason that everything is screened in the order of its occurrence. That is the first principle of perfect illusion—perfect continuity. The second principle is, that all that is essential must occur on the screen, which is the principle of perfect progression. Both the spoken drama and the fiction story permit a development that is contrary to these principles of photodrama. The writer of those forms builds up a fabric of deception, as it were, around the real events that hides the truth and makes it seem as tho it were just the opposite—until the grand surprise at the end. He does this by means of cleverly framed innuendoes, artificial explanations offered by various persons in the play or story and the delay of misleading evidence that is cleared up in speeches and dialog, that in turn explains why they made the mistakes. The photoplay gains power by being more direct.

We do not try to outwit our audiences; we take them into our confidence. If we can do this cleverly and suggestively, we can equal, if not surpass, any of the effects to be obtained by other forms of dramatic expression.

(EXAMPLE 74.) We see a crime about to be committed, but all of the criminal that appears is a hand—possibly scarred—slipping thru the parting of the portières. When the hero who was robbed or assaulted by that hand finds the ring, the audience finds the criminal. Another instance of showing the essential progressive action, but reserving the full disclosure till the climacteric Situation, is found in the finding of a woman's lost boy by the man she loves. Later she is led to believe that the boy has gone the evil way he started for. She comes to the man she had scorned, for help; the man takes her to a boy's school where her boy is the leader. We had only seen the lover find the boy and then we returned to the main line of action.

But are not the audiences' hopes and fears heightened by omniscience? Their knowledge does not mean foreknowledge, by any means. The hero must work out his own salvation and overcome the villain just the same. The fact that they know that the hero is sitting on the box that contains the treasure for which he is looking is a hundred times more dramatic than if they are not told till the end, when the circumstance may be forgotten. The finest Situations are those wherein he does not realize the true state of affairs that the foregoing scene has fully disclosed to the audience.

(EXAMPLE 75.)   In "Madame X" we find the young barrister defending his own mother who has committed murder.   At first neither mother nor son is aware of it.   The audience knows, and this knowledge makes of this scene one of the most powerful Situations in all Drama.

The Close-View—in the capacity of showing only a small portion of the physical action magnified—is most effective in producing Situations.   Again, it brings that to the knowledge of the spectator of which the recipient is blithely ignorant.

(EXAMPLE 76.)   A Close-View shows us the hand of the villain stealing the priceless scarf-pin; or the hero's wallet that means his all.

Or again, the Close-View can bring close what the audience witnesses almost unemotionally from a distance, possibly showing the burglar's ugly face where they saw but a head in the foliage.   The Close-View is, in fact, one of the most effective devices at the command of the playwright.

The Caption, too, is capable of doing service as a Situation, by rousing a thrill in drama just as they rouse a laugh in comedy.   Our difficulty in this relation is to prevent it from

171

robbing the scene, or scenes, to follow of surprise or suspense.

(EXAMPLE 77.) The following strengthens a fact that has half-dawned in the mind of the audience. Without the Caption the fact would have passed without particular notice: "Mrs. Donnelly Handles Dalton's Deadly Messenger, Neither Dreaming That She Is the Intended Victim." Again we impress a Situation that must not be lost sight of: "Marsten Thinks the Mortgage Lost That Has Slipped Into the Lining of the Coat."

Thus we have seen that even infinitesimal, tho important, points may be made potential Situations by bringing them "down front" in the spot-light, or giving them the advantages obtained thru introspection in fiction.

Death in itself is neither dramatic nor a Situation. Drama is dependent on life, struggle and complication; and a Situation may be evolved out of a perilous circumstance in which the character is threatened with death. A Situation always germinates further life-action; death terminates a line of action and eliminates forever an active participant. Death is never the Climax, but the end.

Since Situations are a matter of such consequence to the playwright, it behooves him to harvest them with the same diligence that he garners plot material. He may readily file and classify them under the same captions and sub-divisions as he does his plot material. Again, the same sources of material are available, especially the daily press, which graciously condenses Situations and Climaxes in the large type of its head-lines.

(EXAMPLE 78.) Ten are chosen at random from current newspapers: (1) Bee Upsets Big Auto; (2) Deceived by His Valet; (3) Two Women Claim Boy; (4) Finds Woman Stowaway; (5) Claims Wife— She Laughs; (6) Woman Gives Away Coins (7) Prince Weds a Commoner; (8) President Is Captured; (9) Blind Man Made to See; (10) Identified by X-Ray.

Among the great number of technical terms that photoplaydom has acquired is one identified with literary work-shop slang as well—the "Punch." It is more expressive than elegant, however. The Punch is the Climax and something more. It must first be an effective Climax; secondly, it is the effect of that Climax. The Punch is the momentous event that is the excuse for the play. It is the tremendous moment of revealment, when the dramatic struggle that has waged

173

uncertainly from side to side suddenly pitches forward with the victor for good and all— just as the audience had been schooled either to hope or be afraid that it would. The issue of the Climax-Punch must be sufficient to make the audience literally hold its breath, or emotionally rise to the occasion. It is the thing that hits you square between the eyes with an effect that stuns and lasts. If a play has no Punch, it is not a perfect play.

(EXAMPLE 79.) In "The Coming of the Real Prince," the Climax of the first part was the coming of the bogus prince; the Punch came at the end of play when the real prince came. The first was a city "tin horn Sport"; the second was the plain grocer's boy, who had been Annie's neighbor all her life, and a real prince too—that was the Punch!

The Punch, then, is the motive-idea of the play summed up in a cumulative stroke. It bears the same relation to the story that the climax does to the plot. It is not the big culminating action so much as it is the effect that dawns on the audience. It is the emotional truth of the author's vision come home to dwell in the heart of each one who sees the vision. The Punch is the recognition by the audience of a visible symbol of spiritual struggle.

A successful play must be able to claim an honorable place among the most important emotional experiences of the spectators—Unity and Harmony must have induced exquisite Reality.

CHAPTER V

Unity Plus Harmony Equals Effect

Questions in the mind of the audience; reason; truth; struggle; solution; the title; harmony values.

UNITY resolves itself into a rule of reasonable cause; Harmony becomes solely a matter of consistent effect. Unity has to do with selection, and is a part of the plot; Harmony with arrangement, and is essential to dramatic expression. One is the perfect relation of the parts; the other the perfect expression of the whole.

First of all, there are unities of language that must be observed to insure perspicuity, precision and perfect presentation of the idea.

This demands a command of words, a knowledge of grammar and an exercise of rhetoric. The illiterate writer is beyond imagining and might be compared with a blind painter or a mute singer. The next step toward eventual harmony is the choice of an appropriate idea and a subsequent coherent development. The units of development should not merely stick together; they must *cling* to each other. Thus we fulfill the unities of impression, which is the simpler part of our task.

Perfect unity in expression is harmony. There is a measure, a key, a pitch, a tone— or a color scheme, if you will—that cannot be violated. The main theme is the refrain, or motif, to which we continually hark back, until we build up a volume of melody that releases itself in a grand finale of harmony. We describe a crescendo—tho it is not a perfect arc, in that its highest point is near the end instead of the center, when it descends rapidly to the plane of its beginning. That is the mark of the perfect artistic production: Balance, the last bar pitched in the same keynote as the first! This suggests the entire play in a single effective impression.

(EXAMPLE 80.) In the first scene of "The Master of the Lost Hills," Shelburne receives a letter from Petronella Dupuyster saying that she is jilting him for Baron Komisky. The blow shatters his ideas of women, and he cynically thinks none of them is worth while. . . . In the last scene it is the morning of his coming marriage to Mary. He reads an item in the paper saying Petronella is seeking divorce from her bogus "Baron"; Mary enters and he takes her in his arms, making it clear that he has found THE woman.

Every element must be in unison, then, in the perfect play. The poetic play must be rendered every *artificial* aid available to delineate, identify and appeal to poetic *feeling*. The same is true of romantic, realistic, idealistic, or any other specific type. Each play, for that matter, has its own peculiar exigencies that call for unity auxiliaries for the sake of harmony. The character must have his consistent traits, condition must have its appropriate environment, situations may be heightened by setting, deeds are strengthened by atmosphere—just as the effect is enhanced by harmony. Thus we disclose one of the most vital reasons why the least element in the play should become a factor in the Climax;

why it should contribute to, color, culminate and sustain the desired effect of totality to be left in the mind of the audience.

(EXAMPLE 81.) In "The Lost Melody" we begin with the Caption: "Malcolm Decides to Wait and Make His Proposal to Rosalie an Artistic Occasion." This typifies Malcolm's character that loves to luxuriate in his own dreams. We next find him a collector of rare jewels, of which his business-like rival, Douglas, only realizes the monetary value. The night of the proposal, Rosalie mistakes Malcolm's dreaming for lackadaisical disregard. Douglas seizes the opportunity and proposes. The setting is a glorious, lover-like night. They sing the melody that intoxicates Malcolm and sobers Douglas. When Malcolm has detached himself from his ideal state, he finds Rosalie in Douglas' arms. They part forever. Douglas, true to his type of sordid materialism, rises and falls thru his desire for money. Malcolm becomes the big artist we have felt he might be. And so, till the lost melody is found again, we find a potent strain of harmonizing units building a persistent effect that will haunt the audience after seeing the play.

The literal construction of the photoplay has evolved a method of writing the manuscript that peculiarly lends itself to the composition of dramatic "business." While action is the language of emotion, brevity vivifies action. Terseness is a potential factor, then, in the construction of the manuscript, and there are several ways in which terseness may be suggestively conveyed thru the physical treatment of written action. In this connection, we must bear in mind that verbs are natively *action words;* adjectives are color or quality words; and adverbs are essentially drama words.

(EXAMPLE 82.) A simple analysis of the fiction value of the nine parts of speech reveals that (1) ARTICLE is insignificant and is to be used as little as possible; (2) ADJECTIVE is a quality word that visualizes the image and description cannot do without it; (3) NOUN tells what or who we are talking about; have no more nouns than you want the reader to see objects, and no object unless it is clearly visible; (4) VERB is the action word, the dynamo of emotion, the important word in drama; (5) PRONOUN is he, she or it—nothing more and the noun is always to be used in preference, if its repitition permits; (6) ADVERB is the word of color, manner, time, subtilety, charm and emotion and tells HOW, which is what the reader wants to know; (7) CONJUNCTION joins together qualities, objects, groups and may connect short statements and break long ones; (8) INTERJECTION is the less artful way of expressing emotion; (9) PREPOSITION

is the word of passing, the bridge, pause at it and you have suspense.

The Synopsis, while it does not permit of unctuous detail, yet there seems no reason why it should not follow the rules of all narration and be written tersely, but in full, rounded sentences, instead of in the abbreviated forms suggested for the Scenario.

(EXAMPLE 83.) Some writers employ the comma thruout the entire scene: "Donnelly reading over letter girl has written, scowls, roars for girl," etc. Others use the dash in the same manner: "Donnelly reading letter—scowls—" etc. A more effective way is suggested by the use of the semi-colon and the use of sentences. Each sentence is to mark either all the consecutive action of one character, or the short sequences of action in which possibly all the characters are involved: "Donnelly reading over letter girl has just handed him; scowls; roars for girl; reprimands her brutally. Boy enters; says Dalton is outside; Donnelly shakes his head can't see him; boy says it is urgent. Donnelly nods and turns belligerently to receive Dalton." There is vivacity in the short periods and the reader almost instantly falls into the recurring sequences with perfect understanding.

We come to the conclusion at length that

idea, technique, situation or dramatic atmosphere alone is not the thing, but the *harmony* of all of these. And in attaining this harmony we find that delineation is essential, while description is incidental, for the simple reason that the characters and setting describe themselves the instant they are seen. The physical picture saves all the space fiction devotes to visualization.

There is nothing more distracting to harmony than the method of some directors in accelerating action by means of perpetual short scenes, regardless of the nature of the theme. If used to excess, this continued employment of the Return sinks its subject to the low level of the "chase" picture that was the curse of the early attempts at dramatic depiction. The time will come, it is hoped, when the chase, the crude pantomime and the actor who flirts with the audience, will become taboo just as the telephone dialog, the soliloquy and the aside are avoided in the best spoken dramas. Both the Return and the Flash are merely alternatives to be employed as special devices for special occasions and not stable units upon which the entire play may be built. They are merely effective accelerators of contributive action and secondary to the main theme.

Unity is agreeable accord; harmony is artistic concord. Unity is a perfect assemblage of the parts (seen from the constructive viewpoint); harmony is the spontaneous chord shed by the newly created instrument (felt from its perfect operation). In unity we make the parts absolutely consistent with well-known rules; in harmony we make the whole naturally real according to the principles of life and experience.

Strictly speaking, the photodrama is not governed by the so-called Dramatic Unities, restricting dramatic operation to a single Time, Place and Action. For the photodrama, thru the latitude permitted in its multitudinous scenes, may cover continents and span generations. The old order remains unchanged in the matter of Action—there can be but *one* Action. There is an axiom in drama, however, that applies equally to spoken drama and to screen drama: The nearer a play approximates the actual time consumed in a definite, continuous and centered story that it represents, the more convincing is its effect likely to be. In other words, if the consumation of a deed required exactly fifty minutes in actuality and took fifty minutes to be acted, it would be a perfect unity in point of time. But how rare it is to conceive a deed, every consecutive second of which is dramatically worth while!

Finally we come to the harmonious element that appears first on the manuscript, but is conceived wisely last—the Title. The title must fit the play like a glove, and hide its complete nature as tho it were a glove.

Fortunately, photoplays are not chosen—by either public or producers—because of their titles, as books and short stories are often selected. Yet, because of the seeming lack of importance attached to this part of the play, writers, editors and manufacturers do not always accord it the important place it deserves, and will eventually demand. Good, fitting and perfect titles to plays are a distinct commercial asset, beside being a requisite to artistic and harmonious completeness. The title is the head, the handle, the greeting, the introduction, the pleasing personality, the cue and the bid to favor of the as-yet unread manuscript and the as-yet unseen play. A title should be exquisite—like a finely-carved casket, obviously containing a precious treasure—its exterior suggesting mystery, wonder, and delight that must follow its revealment. The title must suggest the individuality of the play without revealing its identity as shown thru development, climax and denouement.

Unity we may find if we look for it; Harmony cannot be discovered by the keenest critic, for it is not hand-made but born. When the flesh and form of the play is perfectly built, Harmony enters in a breath—it is the soul of the play! Harmony is the last word of drama!

PART IV
FORMS AND TYPES OF THE PHOTOPLAY

Above all things Drama is human—it has its hours for laughing and weeping, for strife and death; it is governed by both free will and destiny—it calls its moods Drama and Melodrama; Comedy and Tragedy.

CHAPTER I

DRAMA AND MELODRAMA; TRAGEDY; COMEDY; OTHER FORMS; "SPLIT REEL"; SHORT PLAY; LONG PLAY; SPECTACLE; ADAPTATIONS; PLAY DIVISIONS.

PHOTOPLAY audiences arrived at a stage of mature understanding and appreciation of the photodrama long before the manufacturers and producers had emerged from the jungle of crudity. The latter are inclined to remain money-makers and not become art producers; they are filling their pockets today from the emptied brains of yesterday and forcing tomorrow to go begging. With few exceptions the plain drama is exaggerated into melodrama, startling the audiences thru the violent acts of the characters, or dynamic spectacle, or extraordinary setting—rather than thru the simple medium of pure dramatic construction that stirs the imagination and sways the emotions with a semblance of real experience. Drama is one of life's exquisite emotional phenomena brought home to an audience thru the pictured experience of others.

Melodrama is easiest to write, since it is all high-lights and black shadows. It demands the concoction of a series of violence and spectacle to happen in a logical and progressive order. Melodrama resembles farce, in that the characters are cursed with all the earmarks of the deepest-dyed type they portray—the beetle-browed villain, or the ludicrous Jew-Irishman-Nigger. In the true drama we meet men and women who live poignantly in our lives—tho we see them for the first time. The melodramatists had things their way because the few artists had no co-operation.

Comedy is most difficult to write, and is easiest to sell—meaning, of course, pure comedy. It is more difficult, for instance, to keep an audience laughing for twenty minutes than it is to keep them in suspense over a dramatic story for an hour or more. The photo-counterpart of the Play of Manners, or the Polite Comedy, is bound to become one of the future developments of the Photo-drama. Photoplay Comedy has been in the hands of the Philistines since its inception. Rarely do we see anything but the rollicking farce. Polite Comedy has its exquisite moments that mingle delighted smiles with pathetic tears; Rollicking Comedy is all wide-mouthed laughter.

If we are careful in distinguishing from its coarser parasite—"slap-stick" farce—we may say that Rollicking Comedy is an art worthy of one's serious effort. There are certain temperaments, however, incapable of comedy in any form. These playwrights are self-conscious of their failing! The Polite Comedy is marked by grace, repression and humor. It is a delicate cameo of the serious drama— only it avoids the villainies, perils and horrors of life, substituting in their place the failings, fantasies and prejudices that are both humorously and pathetically human.

In the Rollicking Comedy, then, *everything must be comical*. The term "everything" is imperative; it means idea, title, plot, every situation, every scene, every insert, every reference, every character, every setting, every action, every suggestion. "It is to laugh!" Comedy demands exhaustive treatment of detail. It is insufficient to say that a character performs an act in a funny way; we must tell in detail how the action is done to make it so funny. Comedy must always be delineated good-naturedly, and never with satire or animus. Misfortune is not a comedy subject.

In all good drama—whether it be drama, melodrama, comedy or tragedy—there must be an idea in the material, a motive in the characterization, a definite end to be attained; a reasonable cause, a logical effect and a climacteric deed; a plot.

In all drama there is struggle with an obstacle. In pure drama and melodrama we have the hero struggling against the obstacles and pitfalls placed in his path by the villain;

in comedy the character struggles against the ludicrous situations that rise in his course; in tragedy evil circumstances overwhelm the hero no matter how heroic his struggles are against them.

The reel, or unit of photoplay length, has both its advantages and its disadvantages. The "Split reel" play is under a disadvantage. If it be only a plotless farce—which it is most frequently—it makes little difference, since that form is only a fragment, or series of them.

There are many ways in which the Short Play—or one-real—may be compared to the Short Story, and the Long Play—or multiple-reel—to the Novel. The Short Play, is intensive in method. We pursue the development swiftly and relentlessly from the opening scene to the culmination.

The Long Play is not a Short Play amplified—as we so often see them padded. It is not in any sense a Short Play told in two or more parts (or reels). Each part (or reel) of the Long Play, like each chapter of the Novel, is a unit in itself, having its own beginning, development and climacteric situation. Yet it is progressive and becomes fragmentary unless considered as an intergral part of the whole production. Each part (or reel) of the Long Play accumulates and takes care of its own situations and complications, which may tend to pile up revelations of dramatic interest to heighten the suspense of the reel to follow, or which may be a direct progressive result of the reel preceding. In the Long Play each reel ends with the introduction of a new complication that necessitates an entirely new line of treatment. It is literally "continued in our next." Each reel must always advance; it never can go backward. In each succeeding reel of the Long Play we find that the story has just received a set-back in its solution, thru the introduction of a new and formidable obstacle that demands another line of solution from that employed in the preceding reel.

(EXAMPLE 84.) In "The Coming of the Real Prince," the first reel ends with the climacteric situation showing our heroine really won heart and soul by the unprincipled villain. But the story cannot end here; common sense and instinct tell us that that is not the culmination of the plot. And sure enough, just as the audience thought the villain was

going to be caught and thrashed perhaps, by the hero —the heroine elopes with the villain! Thus we have the constructive foundation for another reel, that demands an entirely different course of action.

The studios themselves are usually responsible for the thrilling or gorgeous spectacles displaying a wonderful array of scenery, setting, hordes of actors, marvelous mechanism and a hundred other entertaining, and possibly pleasing, features that bear only a distant relationship to bona fide drama. If the manufacturer has a menagerie, a railroad, a thousand pounds of dynamite, a wild west outfit or a military equipment on his hands he naturally desires to make use of it. It is then that the photoplay hack is called upon to write one or more stories "around" it — and they usually are considerably around it and seldom inside of it.

The play offered in the following chapter is an unpretentious example, falling short of perfection in more than one particular, tho equal to the occasion of modestly exemplifying most of the rules and principles set forth in the present work.

191

An Example can but show you what to do and what not to do; it cannot teach you how or why to do a thing; the more perfect it be the less mechanics it will reveal; it is not a lesson to you in Technique, but the result of Technique by another.

CHAPTER II

A Specimen Photoplay

THE EFFECTIVENESS OF TYPOGRAPHY; "THE SALT OF VENGEANCE,"—A SHORT PLAY DRAMA.

TYPOGRAPHICAL display in preparing manuscript will effect its immediate understandability. A careless and unintelligent display will require extra time and patience on the part of the reader to fathom its full significance. A careful and intelligent arrangement will enable the reader to grasp the full meaning of every detail on sight. The special features of the arrangement and display of type adhered to in the following play are: (1) Single-spacing body of Synopsis;

(2) Underlining setting, or location, above the text of scene action; (3) Indenting scene text, single-spacing it and making it stand out as by putting double space before and after it; (4) All Captions and dialog typed in capital letters; (5) Using the red ribbon for all matter that is to appear intact on the screen; (6) Numbering Scenes and Captions in Arabic numerals and Inserts in Roman; (7) Indenting Close-Views double the distance of Scene indentation; (8) In case of more than one reel, numbering the scenes consecutively (1 to 100, etc.) but, after the first reel, putting in parenthesis the number of scenes it represents in current reel, as: Scene 48 (13), always referring back to the serial number on its reappearance. (The foregoing remarks are necessary since print-type gives only the effect without following the rules identically.)

HENRY ALBERT PHILLIPS,
New York City . . . . N. Y.

THE SALT OF VENGEANCE.

A Short Play (One Reel) Drama

In 23 Interior and 17 Exterior Scenes.

By Henry Albert Phillips.

193

Synopsis:

The matter of a rotten bridge is brought to the attention of Donnelly, a penurious railroad president, by Dalton, a conscientious consulting engineer. Donnelly refuses to listen or heed the report. Dalton pleads, insists and finally is discharged.

Dalton does not tell his wife of his misfortune. Failing to get work after two months he is on the verge of a breakdown. His wife has learned the truth and sets out at once with their little boy, Arthur, to her father's for aid. On the way home Dalton reads of the terrible train wreck at the very point he had condemned. Hardly able to think, he hurries home, finding a note from his wife saying that she and the child have taken—the train that was wrecked! More than half-crazed, Dalton hurries to the scene of the wreck.

Mrs. Donnelly, the sweet wife of the president, has learned of the wreck and hurries to the scene to offer air. With her is her own lovable child, Florence. It is her car that carries the terribly maimed little Arthur to the hospital. The child's leg is amputated.

Mrs. Donnelly has kept her identity secret, but continues to bestow every blessing in her power upon the stricken family. Dalton has gone completely mad. There seems but one influence under heaven that makes Arthur want to live, and brings intelligence and peace to Dalton—that is Florence. They worship the wonderful little girl.

Dalton's insanity takes the form of a blind

obsession. He seeks vengeance on Donnelly. He learns that Donnelly has an only child. He immediately sets to work and makes a terrible bomb. He then plans to telegraph for Mrs. Donnelly and her daughter and have the train wrecked and the child blown to atoms on the spot where his child was maimed.

Mrs. Donnelly and Florence are with Arthur when the telegram is brought by a servant, they just catch the fatal train. Meanwhile, Dalton has forcibly entered Donnelly's office, tells him at the point of a gun what will happen in less than an hour and waits. In that hour Donnelly passes thru hell. When there is but twenty minutes left, Dalton espies the picture of Florence, realizes that she is the victim, his mind clears and the men hurry away on the almost hopeless task of rescue.

It is Dalton who arrives alone, half dead, just as the train looms up. They ignore his white signal and he heroically cuts his wrist and saturates the handkerchief with blood that warns the engineer of danger the last instant.

Dalton recovers; the men are reconciled; Dalton gets back his position; Donnelly mends his ways.

(NOTE: *Use another sheet of paper.*)

HENRY ALBERT PHILLIPS,
New York City . . . . N. Y.

THE SALT OF VENGEANCE.

Author's Remarks:

In the explosion scene, the supposed bridge that is blown up could be a set erected to look like portion of bridge showing thru trees. The question of color of the blood is solved by the Caption.

Scene Plot:

INTERIORS	EXTERIORS
Donnelly's Office,	Beneath bridge, 1, 22.
2, 4, 25, 27, 29, 31.	Veranda, 6, 26.
Ante-room,	City street, 12.
3, 8, 10, 20, 24.	Field hospital, 15, 17.
Dalton living-room,	Open field, 14, 16.
5, 7, 9, 11, 13, 21, 28,	Near automobile, 18.
40.	Railway station, 30.
Hospital, 19.	Stretch of railroad,
Telegraph office, 23.	32, 34, 39
Passenger coach, 35.	Another stretch, 33, 37.
Engine cab, 38.	On railway trestle, 36.

Cast:

CHARLES DALTON—Arthur's father; consulting engineer; serious, nervous.

JOHN DONNELLY—Florence's father; railroad president; brutal.

FLORENCE DONNELLY—(Ingenue) Sweet child with wonderful influence.

ARTHUR DALTON—(Juvenile) Injured in accident.

MRS. DALTON—Anxious type.

MRS. DONNELLY—Kindly.

Telegraph Clerk, Newsboy, Stenographer, Employe, two laborers, Engineer, Fireman, Guards, Doctors, Nurse.

A SPECIMEN PHOTOPLAY

(NOTE: *Use another sheet of paper.*)
HENRY ALBERT PHILLIPS,
New York City . . . . N. Y.

THE SALT OF VENGEANCE.

Scenario:

SCENE 1. BENEATH RICKETY RAILROAD BRIDGE.
Dalton making notes; he directs one of two laborers to strike pier of bridge. He does so; there is a hail of debris; they all hurry out in alarm.

CAPTION 1. CONSULTING ENGINEER DALTON BRINGS MATTER OF ROTTEN BRIDGE BEFORE DONNELLY, PRESIDENT OF THE ROAD.

SCENE 2. PRESIDENT DONNELLY'S OFFICE.
Donnelly bullying stenographer over an error. Boy enters; announces Dalton; Donnelly shakes head emphatically can't see him; boy says it is urgent; Donnelly looks at him a second, then nods and turns belligerently to receive Dalton.

SCENE 3. ANTEROOM OF OFFICE.
Dalton pacing determinedly and anxiously. Boy enters; nods; exit Dalton.

SCENE 4. SAME AS 2. OFFICE.
Dalton advances and begins confidently. Donnelly stops him. Dalton amazed; walks to map and points out bridge. Donnelly angrily refuses to listen. Dalton turns; delivers eloquent tirade. Donnelly in rage rings bell; obsequious employe

enters; he is told to put Dalton out and pay him off. Dalton speaks his mind before he goes.

SCENE 5.   DALTON LIVING-ROOM.
Mrs. Dalton sewing a man's shirt; kisses sleeve tenderly; turns in surprise and pleasure as Dalton enters; looks into his eyes; questions him anxiously; looks at clock. He pats her on shoulder and smiles, shaking head; asks for Arthur. They call and child runs in; Dalton takes him in his arms and makes plain his love.

SCENE 6.   VERANDA, DONNELLY MANSION.
Mrs. Donnelly reading to Florence; pauses occasionally to lavish affection; they register approach of motor. Mother sighs; child brightens. Car swings up; Donnelly alights; scolds chauffeur about tire; brushes maid who holds open door; scowls at wife who approaches yearningly; sees child and softens; takes her in his arms.

CAPTION 2.   MRS. DALTON LEARNS THE TRUTH AFTER TWO MONTHS' DECEPTION.

SCENE 7.   SAME AS 5.   LIVING-ROOM.
Dalton leave-taking; marked change in his appearance which he tries to hide from wife. He looks at clock saying it is time he was at office; kisses her and child; exit. Mrs. Dalton looks after him, then turns resolutely to telephone.

SCENE 8.   SAME AS 3.   ANTEROOM OF OFFICE.
Same boy as in 2 at switchboard; looks up name

*in book; same employe as in 4. Passes thru;
pantomimes throwing person out bodily at boy's
question; boy shakes head emphatically and
bangs up receiver.*

SCENE 9. SAME AS 5. LIVING-ROOM.
*Mrs. Dalton staggering back from telephone;
sinks into chair and takes Arthur tragically into
her arms.*

SCENE 10. ANOTHER OUTER OFFICE.
*Dalton pacing up and down; another man enters;
men shake hands cordially; Dalton asks question; other points to empty desks; Dalton turns
sadly away.*

SCENE 11. SAME AS 5. LIVING-ROOM.
*Mrs. Dalton and Arthur dressed for journey;
bag on table; she is finishing note; holds it up
and reads:*

INSERT (1) LETTER. "FATHER WILL HELP
US OUT, DEAR, AND I AM TAKING AR-
THUR TO HOYTSVILLE WITH ME."

SCENE 11. (CONTINUED.)
*She has Arthur kiss note; she kisses it, sticks it
in the mirror; exeunt.*

SCENE 12. CITY STREET.
*Dalton going along despondent; boy asks him
to buy paper. Dalton brushes him away; boy
insists, pointing excitedly to scare head. Dalton
shows wild interest;*

INSERT (II) *News head,* TERRIBLE TRAIN WRECK. HOYTSVILLE LOCAL PLUNGES THRU FAULTY TRESTLE.

SCENE 12. (CONTINUED.)
Dalton devours news; boy demands payment and he absently hands him coin; boy offers change, but he moves away, paying no attention.

SCENE 13. SAME AS 5. LIVING-ROOM.
Enter Dalton still reading; pauses; realizes no one is there to welcome him; shrugs shoulders and sits down shaking his head; suddenly espies note in mirror; seizes it with a look of apprehension; reads, falling back in chair and clutching his hair; rises unsteadily; gropes his way out his face contorted in agony.

CAPTION 3. MRS. DONNELLY INCOGNITO OFFERS AID.

SCENE 14. STRETCH OF ROAD. (Train wreck and field hospital visible.)
Crowd held back by guards, evidently railroad employes. Donnelly car drives on; Mrs. Donnelly orders car stopped and alights, inquiring the trouble; face convulsed in horror; asks guard to let her pass; he refuses; she shows pass; he takes off his hat and sends one of men with her.

SCENE 15. FIELD HOSPITAL NEAR SCENE OF WRECK.
Mrs. Dalton on stretcher in foreground; she becomes conscious; cries for Arthur. But everyone seems to be working over form on cot a few feet

*away; a doctor steps aside; Mrs. Dalton screams
and creeps toward them; falls, fainting as she
clasps a limp little hand; Arthur is revealed to
audience. Doctor turns to companion.*

INSERT (III) DIALOG. "WE MUST OPERATE
IMMEDIATELY!"

SCENE 15. (CONTINUED.)
*One doctor has opened case; stands scratching
his head in despair; instrument missing.*

SCENE 16. SAME AS 14. ROADWAY.
*Guards pushing back the curious. Dalton, now
completely mad, enters hatless and wild-eyed;
looks about till he sees people on beds; gives a
cry and tries to pass; guards pushes him back.
Dalton beats down guard murderously; rushes on.*

SCENE 17. SAME AS 15. FIELD HOSPITAL.
*Mrs. Dalton on her knees sobbing before pallet.
Doctor is telling Mrs. Donnelly of predicament;
she instantly points to car; doctor calls his aid
and instantly the cot is lifted and hurried away,
Mrs. Donnelly supporting Mrs. Dalton from
scene.*

SCENE 18. VERY NEAR DONNELLY CAR.
*Florence standing alongside and looking pain-
fully at what is approaching. Men enter with
stretcher. They are halted this moment by appearance of Dalton who lifts cover from Arthur's
face and sobs like a child. The two women appear. A terrible look of frenzy comes into*

201

Dalton's eyes; it gradually disappears as he feels Florence's hand in his; she soothes him completely. Mrs. Dalton is helped into car that drives away. A buggy nearby is requisitioned; they all get in and exeunt.

CAPTION 4. FLORENCE BECOMES THE DALTONS' ANGEL OF HAPPINESS.

SCENE 19. HOSPITAL PRIVATE ROOM.

Arthur in bed; opens his eyes and speaks; nurse motions toward door; Mrs. Dalton enters; Arthur half turns away to mother's great grief. Dalton enters listlessly; maniacal cunning in his eye; in turn, he is almost repulsed by Arthur. Florence enters with bouquet; tiptoes to downcast parents; her influence marked, especially on Dalton; she puts her arm round both of their necks and kisses them in turn. She moves to bedside; Arthur looks up and smiles immediately; she strokes the hand he puts out; kisses his cheek and moves away. Dalton now sobbing takes her in his arms, showing great affection. They all exeunt on tiptoe.

CAPTION 5. SEEKING TERRIBLE VENGEANCE DALTON LEARNS THAT DONNELLY TOO HAS A CHILD.

SCENE 20. SAME AS 3. ANTEROOM.

Dalton conversing with boy to latter's discomfiture; asks cunningly, pointing toward Donnelly's private office, if he has children. Boy

annoyed nods and indicates height of child. Dal-
ton persists; finally boy writes Donnelly's coun-
try home address on piece of paper; Dalton
stowes it away with vicious delight and sneaks
out. Donnelly enters hurriedly; tells boy never
to let Dalton in again.

CAPTION 6. THE MESSENGER OF DESTRUC-
TION AND ITS UNSUSPECTED VICTIMS.

SCENE 21. SAME AS 5. LIVING-ROOM.
Arthur in reclining chair; crutches beside him.
Dalton in corner working on obvious bomb with
time clock connection; looks around crazily now
and then, gathering the outfit in his arms when
he thinks he hears someone coming. Mrs. Dalton
pats him gently when he shows violence toward
an unseen enemy. Enter Florence; Dalton is
first to see her; takes her in his arms joyfully;
changed at once. Florence plays with machine;
he shows how it operates; imitates train; points
to clock; then pantomimes big explosion. They
have not heard Mrs. Donnelly enter; she comes
forward and picks it up; but he is suspicious and
will say no more. Mrs. Dalton draws her gently
away; two shake their heads sadly; approach
Arthur.

CAPTION 7. THE 4.29 TRAIN DOOMED!

SCENE 22. SIMILAR TO 1. BENEATH RAILROAD
BRIDGE.
Dalton's face slowly emerges from bushes; now

hideously maniacal; opens valise and hurriedly arranges mechanism of bomb; clock in plain view; connects wires already strung; hears a noise and crawls away grinning fiendishly.

SCENE 23. TELEGRAPH OFFICE.
Dalton enters; takes folded telegram from pocket; hands it to clerk who opens and reads:

INSERT (IV). MRS. JOHN DONNELLY,
MANORVIEW.
YOUR HUSBAND INJURED—COME AND BRING CHILD—WILL MEET YOU ON TRAIN LEAVING 4.29.
DR. SAVAGE.

SCENE 23. (CONTINUED.)
Clerk looks up skeptically; points to signature; he nods with a frown; he pays and hurries out.

SCENE 24. SAME AS 3. ANTEROOM.
Boy reading; registers bell; shakes his fist at it; reluctantly shuffles thru door other than that marked "President." Enter Dalton cautiously; hurries to and thru president's door; boy returns; puzzled at finding no one; resumes reading.

SCENE 25. SAME AS 2. DONNELLY'S OFFICE.
Enter Dalton, softly locking door; Donnelly alone at desk; does not look up; Dalton throws key thru window as Donnelly looks up; covers him with revolver as he rises angrily; Donnelly startled at something he sees in Dalton's eyes, sits down; reaches for button; Dalton stops him

and makes him move chair from desk; places two photographs in his hand; he glowers at them.

INSERT (V) CLOSE-VIEW PHOTOGRAPHS.
One showing little Arthur smiling and healthy. Other of him emaciated; face disfigured; on crutches, with but one leg.

SCENE 25. (CONTINUED.)
Dalton now convulsed with madness has taken rope from pocket; springs on Donnelly; there is an uncertain struggle in process as scene fades.

SCENE 26. SAME AS 6. VERANDA.
Maid returning telegram to messenger and urging him to follow disappearing auto; he rides away as fast as he can.

SCENE 27. SAME AS 2. OFFICE.
Dalton sits facing Donnelly whom he has bound and gagged; both men with clothes half torn off. Dalton approaches pointing to photographs; tries to speak; breaks down and weeps like a child. Donnelly merely indifferent and defiant. Dalton pantomimes tragically the whole story; beats his breast, points accusingly at Donnelly; raises his clenched fists as tho to brain him; then remembers and smiles crazily; whispers behind his hand:

INSERT (VI) DIALOG. "IN 50 MINUTES YOUR CHILD WILL BE ON THE SCRAP-HEAP, TOO!"

SCENE 27. (CONTINUED.)
*Instant change in Donnelly who rises horror-
struck; searches the maniac's face with terrible
anxiety. Dalton begins to laugh exultantly.*

SCENE 28. SAME AS 5. LIVING-ROOM.
*Mrs. Donnelly has just entered with Florence
with packages which they put on table before
Arthur; it is a big iced cake and delicacies;
Florence claps her hands and kisses boy; Mrs.
Dalton admiring. Messenger interrupts; at first
too exhausted to speak; Mrs. Donnelly takes
telegram; nods; tears it open; half faints; hands
it to Mrs. Dalton who is amazed at her identity.
She comforts Mrs. Donnelly, who seizes Florence; hurries out. Florence kissing flower Arthur has given her.*

SCENE 29. SAME AS 2. OFFICE.
*Shocking change in Donnelly; hair almost white;
jaw sagging as he slumps in seat. Dalton points
malignantly to time with gun; gives way to terrible memory. Donnelly now turns supplicat-
ingly; pleads; weeps. Dalton laughs tauntingly.
Donnelly makes a furious but futile effort; curses
gnashes his teeth; tries to cry out. Dalton
springs to door menacing it with gun.*

SCENE 30. RAILROAD STATION.
*Mrs. Donnelly and Florence anxiously clamber
aboard train.*

SCENE 31. SAME AS 2. OFFICE.
Donnelly now exhausted and still more terribly

changed; hair matted on brow; all arrogance burnt out of him; brutality gone. Dalton now walking about room in a ferment; suddenly pauses before a photograph of Florence on bookcase; pleasure comes in his eyes; he kisses it. Suddenly he springs back; pain in his eyes; a shudder passing over him. Horror in his eyes as he extends portrait toward Donnelly.

INSERT (VII). CLOSE-VIEW PHOTOGRAPH of Florence; Dalton's twitching thumb grasping it.

SCENE 31. (CONTINUED.)
Dalton's face has lost its madness and has become like Donnelly's; he approaches Donnelly, his gun falling to the floor; he tries to speak; Donnelly nods; like a flash he unties Donnelly; the two men look into each other's face an instant; then grasp each other's hand, making it plain that they forgive; they rush to the door which they tear and break down after desperate effort.

SCENE 32. STRETCH OF RAILROAD.
Train speeding along.

SCENE 33. STRETCH OF RAILROAD WITH HIGHWAY ALONGSIDE.
(Be sure to have auto moving toward train.) Follow swaying, madly-driven car containing Donnelly and Dalton. Obvious explosion of tire; auto stops; both spring out in dismay.

Show futility; rush despairingly to track; suddenly Dalton points ahead with a glad cry; a hand car is on a siding close by; laborer tries to stop them from seizing car and is thrown down the embankment; they propel it away.

SCENE 34. STRAIGHTAWAY STRETCH OF RAILWAY.
(Following car.) Both men working in half exhaustion; suddenly Donnelly collapses and pitches off the side of the car. Dalton tries in vain to push car alone up steep incline; seeing the futility he too drops off exhausted; is up again and runs on.

SCENE 35. INTERIOR OF PASSENGER COACH.
Florence and Mrs. Donnelly in foreground; Florence seeing her mother weeping asks her to kiss the flower Arthur gave her; both smile.

SCENE 36. STRETCH OF RAILWAY TRESTLE.
Dalton making his way groggily over it in dangerous manner; looks down once while resting and draws away in horror, realizing that dynamite is there; glances at watch; registers the singing of the rails; hurries on in terror.

CAPTION 9. DALTON SEVERS HIS WRIST TO MAKE THE BLOOD-RED DANGER SIGNAL.

SCENE 37. CURVE OF RAILROAD.
Dalton has fallen at last between the tracks; structure (artificial) of bridge may be seen several hundred feet behind; train plainly in sight

bearing down on him. He has been waving his handkerchief weakly with no effect; shakes his head and with frantic weakness gets out his knife; severs his wrist; presses handkerchief.

SCENE 38. ENGINE CAB.
Cab swaying; fireman leans over frantically signalling to engineer to down brakes; engineer pulls throttle back and both jump down.

SCENE 39. SAME AS 37. RAILROAD.
Dalton, his arm still raised waveringly; streams of blood running down it; he collapses. Mrs. Donnelly and Florence among first passengers to appear. Doctor comes forward and tourniquets arm. They are all startled by tremendous explosion that sends debris up in a cloud; supposed bridge collapses. All turn thankfully to Dalton.

CAPTION 9. THE BALM OF VENGEANCE.

SCENE 40. SAME AS 5. LIVING ROOM.
Dalton sleeping in chair, his arm in bandage; Florence enters; signals someone; Donnelly enters tenderly carrying Arthur; Dalton opens his eyes; sees Donnelly caressing his boy; Donnelly turns; they look at each other and smile; Florence takes her father's hand and puts it into Dalton's. (Fade.)

THE END.

GLOSSARY

GLOSSARY

To listen continually to words you do not understand, is Ignorance; to use words persistently and inaccurately, is Pedantry; to essay the Business of Expression and not study the significance of its terminology, is Dabbling.

THE MOST-USED TERMS DEFINED WITH MANY SUGGESTIONS FOR REVISION AND ALTERNATIVE TERMS.

IT was but natural that photoplaydom should be all cluttered up with the crude material from the workshop where it first saw the light of the screen—the Studio-Factory. The Photoplay, step by step, was manufactured. Ideas, pictures, crude plays and even playwrights were manufactured! Let the factory have its own terminology, but do not cripple technique with it. That day has past forever, but we have many of the relics still remaining, most noticeable are those to be found among the terms applied to the technique of the photodrama. They all smack of the factory. There was never a question of literary quality, value or significance. Many of them are unique in their homely appropriateness and should remain. Others are ridiculous and should be changed. Among the latter are terms that are without reason, and which are used with different significance in different studios. There should be a dignified standard of universal usage and recognition. With this aim in view, several suggestions are offered.

Action—Specific act of a character; the Scenario; the combined elements that compose a drama.

Business—The playwright's instructions to the actor to perform the expressive acts that transform him into a character.

Bust — (Meaningless, misleading.) See CLOSE-VIEW.

Caption—The interpretive reading line preceding a Scene, or Sequence, that explains, excites interest and indicates passage of time.

Close-Up—(Unliterary; confusing because of both verbal and adverbal use.) See CLOSE-VIEW.

Climax—The supreme moment in the play; the end toward which all elements tend in the Plot.

Cut-Back—(Really instruction in manufacturing to cut film and go back; misleading to playwright who goes only forward.) See RETURN.

Censor—Person employed by National or Local Board of Censorship to criticize plays with a view to their moral influence.

Chase—An inartistic device in which many scenes are consumed in showing the pursuit of one or more characters by others, and their perilous or ludicrous difficulties.

Close-View—The isolated, microscopic or magnified close view of some important fragment of action or essential piece of evidence or reading matter.

Co-Incidence—A chance incident, meeting or discovery that conveniently helps out the plot and is obviously unconvincing to the audience.

Crisis—The instant that follows the "planting" of a Situation and precedes the Solution; the turning-point when something must happen.

Characters—What the actors should become in the eyes of the audience.

Cast—The list of names, parts and required characteristics of the characters (in some cases includes names of actors taking the parts).

Dissolve—To dissolve one scene or character gradually into another.

Director—The person or persons who translate the playwright's manuscript into action, setting and effects by directing the production of the play, which is simultaneously photographed.

Discover—Means to find a character already upon a scene when it is thrown upon the screen: "Douglas discovered at window."

Denouement—That part of the Plot left after the Climax; the part of the play following the culmination, when "just deserts" are meted out as a result of the foregoing action.

Dynamic—The visible exercise of force, violence and physical effects, as opposed to visualized emotion.

Enter—Said of a character as he enters a scene: "Enter Douglas."

Exit—(Plural EXEUNT.) Said of a character as he leaves a scene: "Exit Douglas."

Establish—To make certain the relationship of a character with other characters and with his surroundings, or to make known his identity.

Episode—An isolated incident not bearing upon the climax which has no place in the Play.

Editor—Person who reads manuscripts to determine their availability, and possibly edits, revises and rebuilds promising manuscripts to practicability.

Exterior—A scene laid actually or presumably in the open-air.

Film—The celluloid strip upon which the photographs are to be—or have been—portrayed. (FILM as a verb seems almost eligible because of usage.)

Fade—To cause a scene to fade gradually into blackness.

Flash—(Variously used by different Companies.) Accurately, when referring to a scene fragment that is flashed for a second on the screen.

Farce—Extravagant Comedy.

Harmony—The perfect agreement, consistency and balance of all the parts with the whole in a complete, artistic and gratifying effect.

Insert—Any matter that breaks the continuity of a scene; printed matter, letters, inscriptions, captions, dialog, close-views, visions and devices other than action.

Interior—A scene laid under the roof and within the four walls of any structure.

Jump—A gap, not merely in the continuity, but in the progressive action of the Play.

Leader—(Prominent editorial in a news-paper.) See CAPTION.

Lead—One of the "star" actors having the leading part in a Play.

Locale—The combined Settings for the main theme of the Play, including Atmosphere.

Long Play—A Play occupying more than one Reel.

Multiple Reel—(See LONG PLAY.)

Manuscript—The written form of the play-wright, containing Synopsis, Cast, Scene-Plot, Remarks and Scenario.

Pantomime—Sign language and inter-com-munication between characters.

Punch—An effective Climax; the effect upon the audience of the Climax.

Plot—The organized dramatic material upon which the Play is elaborated.

Properties—All articles necessary for the ef-fective staging of a play.

Reel—1,000 feet of film; length of a Short Play; the spool upon which the film is wound.

Register—The method of visualizing sounds by showing the reflex action of recipient.

Release—To place a Play upon the market; the Play so released.

Screen—The framed surface upon which the Play is projected; the act of projecting.

Spectacle—A Scene or Play or series showing daring deeds, gorgeous settings or dynamic force or numbers; not necessarily dramatic.

Set—Specific Scene artifically constructed.

Short Play—A one-reel, one-part Play; comparable to the Short Story, or One-act Play.

Setting—The scenic environment in which the action takes place.

Scenario—The Action of a Play laid out in progressive Scenes with appropriate Business.

Synopsis—A condensed version of the play in story form and present tense.

Script—(Slang, by which nothing is gained but ill-repute.) See MANUSCRIPT.

Sequence—Logical order of succession of events; a connected series of incidents.

Serio-Comic—Comedy written in vein of seriousness that makes it ridiculous.

Split Reel—A subject, or Play, occupying less than one reel.

Scene—All the Action in one Setting taken wthout moving or stopping the camera; a Scene broken by any form of Insert is "continued," technically unbroken after the interruption.

Stage—The Cinema stage never exceeds in limits the range of the camera.

Sub-Title—(A secondary title, as: "St. Valentine's Day, or The Fair Maid of Perth," "The Fair Maid of Perth" being the sub-title to "St. Valentine's Day.")   See CAPTION.

Title—The name by which the Play is called and known.

Technique—The science of giving established and effective photoplay form to the dramatic Plot.

Theme—The main line of Plot development; the subject-idea of the Play.

Tint—To color the scene to represent moonlight, lamplight, firelight.

Unity—The agreement and appropriateness of the elements that constitute a Play.

Visualize—To interpret the playwright's ideas in such a way that the audience will see and understand them.

Vision—The screening of some remembered or contemplated action bearing on the play that is passing thru the mind of a character; picturing a dream.